Otto Wagner, 1912, perspective drawing of the second Villa Wagner (Map Guide no 2) from Hüttelbergstrasse (Historisches Museum, courtesy Waissenberger).

treatment of the Künstlerhaus exterior created city-wide beacons of its two central themes: the 'dream' in the gilded figure of Klimt's 'Medicine' and the 'reality' in a pink-red tower of the Karl-Marx-Hof.

These like the other installations were executed by a team from my office under the leadership of Franz Madl. The full sequence of 'chapters' comprising the show was as follows:

- The Makart Procession of 1879
- The Vienna World's Fair and the stockmarket crash of 1873
- The triumph of Strauss' operetta *Die Fledermaus* in 1874
- The Ringstrasse
- Social Democracy from the Hainfelder Party Rally of 1889 to 1913
- Theodor Herzl, his book *The Jewish State* of 1896, and anti-semitism
- Literary life around Karl Kraus' *Die demolierte Literatur* of 1897
- 1899: Karl Lueger's 'politics of communalisation'
- *The Interpretation of Dreams*, 1900: Sigmund Freud and psycho-analysis
- 1902: Otto Wagner
- 1903: The Wiener Werkstätte and Josef Hoffmann
- Arnold Schönberg as a painter, and the Kammersymphonie of 1906
- Robert Musil's *Confusion of the pupils of Törless*
- 1904: Gustav Klimt's Beethoven Frieze
- The Vienna Secession, the Stilkunst, the Kunstschau, Schiele, Kokoschka et al
- 1909: Adolf Loos' Michaelerplatz building and his *Chicago Tribune* tower
- 1914-1918: *The Last Days of Mankind*, the First World War, and the end of the monarchy and the founding of the republic
- 1919: Ludwig Wittgenstein's *Tractatus logico-philosophicus*
- Socialist Vienna and the Housing Construction Act of 1923
- Max Reinhardt and the Josefstadt, the International Exhibition of Theatre Technique, 1923
- 1925-27: *Wozzeck* and *Jonny spielt auf*
- *The Café Elecktric* of 1927 and Viennese silent film
- The world economic crisis of 1929.

The exhibition plans on page 16 show how these elements were presented within the Künstlerhaus building.

HANS HOLLEIN RECONSTRUCTIONS AND MODELS
■ IN THE EXHIBITION ■

MODELS ARE OFTEN USED IN ARCHITECTURE BECAUSE they make it very easy to visualize a given building or urban planning scheme, but they are also good metaphors for themes and concepts or for people and personalities. In an exhibition like this one they are invaluable for making the historical situation come alive. They provide a visual, rather than a verbal explanation of the facts.

It would be satisfying to be able to use period models and original artefacts throughout such a show, but this is rarely possible. Often an original work has been lost or destroyed; sometimes it cannot be moved. Sometimes no model was ever made. When an original was not available for reasons of this kind, and where the 'aura' of age and authenticity was not indispensible to the record, we made reconstructions. Models made in this spirit were not copies but new originals, seen as a recapturing of something thought lost.

Models also have the merit of longevity. They not only enrich the exhibition whilst it is running; they represent something of substance that continues to have value when it is over. The models in this show will be used in the future Vienna Architecture Museum.

Another lasting bonus of the modelmaking process is the new knowledge it gives us of buildings that are lost. Many have never been fully documented and the modelmaking process demands that we patiently piece them together again, from whatever black-and-white photographs remain and from the sketchiest of other details.

Basically there were two types of model in this show. Firstly, full size reconstructions of buildings and artefacts that have been completely destroyed. Secondly, scale models, usually at 1:50 of buildings and urban planning schemes that are still extant in whole or in part.

The documentation which formed the basis of the reconstructions was in each case done by a specialist in the relevant field, with my own architectural office coordinating the projects and overseeing manufacture. This latter stage was the particular responsibility of Erich Pedevilla. Manufacture was made possible by the continuing tradition of excellence in handicrafts in Austria, although there were of course difficulties. Often components which would originally have been made serially by mass-production techniques had to be replicated today by complicated one-off processes somewhat unnatural to their original conception.

The guiding principle of all this reconstruction work was that we should be as faithful as possible to the nature and materials of the original. Where details were not absolutely clear, experts were called in, in several cases from abroad. All buildings were modelled and reconstructed as they were immediately after initial construction, eliminating later changes except where these were known to have been features authorised almost immediately by the architect himself.

I thought it important to have some architectural items full-size in the show, to convey the full dimensions of an architectural work. For this the projects chosen had to be not only classics of the architect's oeuvre, but of suitable original scale. For Otto Wagner I chose the portal to the *Die Zeit* telegraph agency: it had been destroyed, and sparingly but usefully documented. It seemed an important candidate for reconstruction. For Adolf Loos the entrance elevation of the Kärntner Bar was an almost automatic choice, and after the exhibition has finished touring it will be reapplied to the bar, which is still extant internally, to restore its original appearance on the street.

Josef Hoffmann is represented by a reconstruction of the room he created for Gustav Klimt's Beethoven Frieze at the XIV Secessionist Exhibition of 1902. This was probably not the most representative Hoffmann work one could have chosen, but it fitted perfectly to the larger theme of this particular exhibition as an example of the *Gesamtkunstwerk*: of art and architecture integrally combined into one design.

The reconstruction of the Beethoven room
The particular occasion for the 1902 Secessionist show was the completion by Max Klinger of a statue of Beethoven. It was a polychromatic work comprising different marbles and other materials. As the original photos and plan of the exhibition show, it stood as a centrepiece under the main dome of the Secession building. All other contributions to the show – ranging from small wall-reliefs to major wall-paintings and friezes – paid homage to Klinger and Beethoven. Gustav Klimt's frieze on themes from Beethoven's 9th Symphony was generally acknowledged to be the best work.

Hoffmann designed the room in which Klimt's frieze was exhibited, as he did all the other major rooms. He also contributed two sopraportas of his own design to the room. The eventual opening of the show was somewhat delaye from the initial plans, so it is likely that both

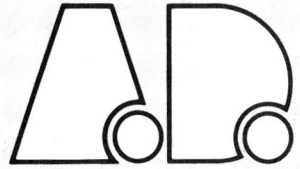

Architectural Design Vol 55 No 11/12

Editorial Offices: 42 Leinster Gardens, London W2 Telephone: 01-402 2141 Subscriptions: 7/8 Holland Street London W8

EDITOR
Dr Andreas C Papadakis
HOUSE EDITOR: Frank Russell
CONSULTANTS: Catherine Cooke, Dennis Crompton, Terry Farrell, Kenneth Frampton,
Charles Jencks, Heinrich Klotz, Leon Krier, Robert Maxwell, Demetri Porphyrios, Colin Rowe, Derek Walker

Architectural Design Profile 61

VIENNA DREAM AND REALITY

A CELEBRATION OF THE HOLLEIN INSTALLATIONS FOR THE EXHIBITION 'TRAUM UND WIRKLICHKEIT WIEN 1870-1930' IN THE KÜNSTLERHAUS VIENNA
GUEST EDITED BY HANS HOLLEIN AND CATHERINE COOKE

Concepts underlying presentation of the exhibition	Hans Hollein	2
Reconstructions and models in the exhibition	Hans Hollein	4
Design for sale: shops of the Wiener Werkstätte	Catherine Cooke	8
Vienna: painting at the turn of the century	Robert Waissenberger	10
Dream and Reality: the Hollein installations	Catherine Cooke	15
The Austrian Werkbund	Stuart Durant	66
Map Guide: Vienna 1870-1930	Catherine Cooke	72

Designed by Catherine Cooke
Covers based on a design specially done for AD by Hans Hollein

For their help in preparation of this Profile, AD is particularly grateful to Madame Nele Haas-Stoclet, for photographs of Werkstätte items in her collection, and for her kind permission to publish them; to Hofrat Dr Robert Waissenberger, Director of the Historical Museum of the City of Vienna, and to Professor Hans Hollein and the staff of his office for allowing us to select and publish photographic materials from his files on the exhibition, and for their generous cooperation.
Where not otherwise credited, all photographs are courtesy of Hans Hollein. With the exception of those otherwise credited, all colour photographs of the Traum und Wirklichkeit exhibition are by Georg Riha, Vienna.

© 1986 AD Editions Ltd. All rights reserved. No part of this publication may be reproduced or transmitted in any form or by any means, electronic or mechanical, including photocopying, recording or any information storage or retrieval system without permission in writing from the Publisher. Neither the Editor nor AD Editions hold themselves responsible for the opinions expressed by writers of articles or letters in this magazine. The Editor will give careful consideration to unsolicited articles, photographs and drawings; please enclose a stamped addressed envelope for their return (if required). Payment for material appearing in AD is not normally made except by prior arrangement. All reasonable care will be taken of material in the possession of AD and agents and printers, but we regret that we cannot be held responsible for any loss or damage. Subscription rates for 1986 (including p&p): Annual rate: UK only £45.00, Europe £55.00, Overseas US$85.00 or UK sterling equiv. Student rates: UK only £39.50, Europe £49.50. Overseas US$75.00 or UK sterling equiv. Double issues £7.95/US$19.95. Single issues £3.95/US$7.95. Please add £1.00/US$2.00 per issue ordered for p&p. All 1986 subscribers will receive Art & Design as part of their subscription. Printed in Great Britain by G A Pindar & Son Ltd, London. [ISSN: 0003-8504]

HANS HOLLEIN
CONCEPTS UNDERLYING PRESENTATION OF THE EXHIBITION DREAM AND REALITY ■ VIENNA 1870-1930 ■

THE IDEA FOR THIS EXHIBITION CAME OUT OF LONG discussions about the need for an exhibition on this very important period in Vienna itself, where full use could be made of the city's resources. It would be an exhibition in Vienna about Vienna.

The concept was elaborated with the help of Robert Waissenberger, Director of the Historical Museum of the City of Vienna, whose staff were responsible for the historical research. Not wanting it to be purely an exhibition about 'the turn of the century', we took a broader period of sixty years, in which developments germane to that central period could be examined more completely. It was of course difficult and somewhat problematic to break down a continually evolving process into precisely defined periods of time, nevertheless there were certain clear contours to the period and certain clear breaks.

It was another fundamental premise that the exhibition should not concentrate exclusively on one single stylistic trend, but should attempt to incorporate a broader range of the ideas current across all the major arts. Thus architecture and city planning were to be given as much consideration as music, drama and film. Equally integral were the intellectual, scientific and political trends which characterised the 'Vienna' phenomenon.

Plainly there had to be omissions, and some themes were better suited than others to the visual presentation which is the basis of the exhibition as a medium. The story was therefore broken down into twenty-four themes or 'chapters', each of which focused on a significant event, a seminal idea or the work and impact of a particular person.

The exhibition was targetted at the broad public, at visitors with greatly varying educational backgrounds and interests. It was aimed as much at the inhabitants of Vienna itself as at tourists. And although historically accurate, it had also to be popular and lively. Original materials were used not only for their 'aura', their authenticity, but for their ability to provoke associations, to communicate complex relationships. Rationality was to stand side-by-side with emotion.

We sought to communicate not just information, but an atmosphere – an atmosphere hinting at the spirit of the epoch. The exhibition's title, Dream and Reality (Traum und Wirklichkeit) was intended to suggest a complex dialectic, a collage-like confrontation and collision. The bloodstained uniform in which Franz-Ferdinand was murdered at Sarajevo is positioned opposite Klimt's 'Kiss'. In one movement the eye can bring together Egger-Lienz's 'Nameless Ones', Winterhalter's portrait of Empress 'Sissi', and Klimt's Beethoven Frieze. Looking from the exhibit on the Karl-Marx-Hof – with the sounds of Mahler's Fifth Symphony in one's ears – there is Hanak's 'Burning People'. Sigmund Freud's consulting couch and Wittgenstein's Tractatus address each other across the period as two poles of intellectual inspiration. Marlene Dietrich stretches her leg for the first time and adjusts her stocking, and the eroticism of Klimt and Schiele hangs like a heavy perfume over the whole exhibition, penetrating every room and space. The opulence of Makart, master of the grandiose entry, leads abruptly into the cool, objective atmosphere of Otto Wagner's work. As Wagner created richly Byzantine effects, special street cars were ferrying corpses to the central cemetery for two million people. The dream and the reality. These street cars (and the gas, electricity and water-works), were already in municipal ownership. Burgermeister Lueger stook up opposite the Emperor and opened the door onto a socialist Vienna which was not to be realised.

The condition of the Jews in Vienna is inevitably a major theme of the exhibition. Hitler's Mein Kampf lies open at his discussion of 'the Vienna problem', amidst the Zionist writings of Theodor Herzl. Karl Kraus' Last Days of Mankind documents that mankind which cried its opposition to Loos' building on the Michaelerplatz; which sat in his Kärntner Bar – its front reconstructed full-size here in the original materials – or which purchased fine accoutrements, by Josef Hoffmann perhaps, from the Wiener Werkstätte's shops. It was Hoffmann who would create the artistic apotheosis of the period, but it would be in Brussels not in Vienna. His Palais Stoclet is represented by a new model and by Klimt's cartoons for the great dining room frieze.

As an exhibition it contains concrete objects, but they are also metaphors; metaphors of a dream which became reality, and of a reality that no-one dreamt of. Through its city-planning dimension the exhibition was not confined even to the city centre, far less to the Künstlerhaus itself. Its manifestations stand throughout Vienna, and the

Documentary photographs of Wagner's portal for *Die Zeit*, **left**, and Loos' Kärntner Bar facade, **right**. Exhibition reconstruction of the former, see page 23, by Otto Kapfinger and latter, page 49, by Herman Czech.

Hoffmann's room and his sopraportas date from the previous year, 1901.

Set into the walls underneath Klimt's frieze were decorative panels by Rudolf Jettmar, Othmar Schimkowitz, Leopold Stolba, Richard Luksch, Friedrich König, Emil Orlik, Maximilian Lenz, Ernst Stöhr and Koloman Moser. In front of the pillar, as seen in the photograph here, was a small freestanding marble sculpture – Klinger's 'Mädchenkopf' (Girl's Head).

Central to the overall architectural concept was the view through three large openings to the main hall where Klinger's 'Beethoven' stood. Josef Hoffmann wrote in the exhibition catalogue:
'In order to fulfill their function and provide a framework worthy of the central feature of the exhibition, Klinger's 'Beethoven', the exhibition rooms had to maintain the air of monumentality. Given our limited means and our obvious duty to use only genuine materials throughout – to avoid any pretence or lying – it was imperative to observe the greatest simplicity in both materials and the language of form. The most appropriate solution was to apply a coating of rough plaster to the walls...The alteration of the rough surfaces with the smooth produced the architectural ordering of the walls. The grandeur (lit: costliness) of the rooms had to come exclusively from the artistic value of the painted and plastic decoration. All the more assertive elements of this decoration were placed on the two side walls, in order to give the central room the calm desired for enjoyment of the main work. The two side halls open onto the central hall, thus increasing its significance and ensuring that the visitor comes to the statue somewhat prepared.'

Gustav Klimt wrote in the catalogue about his frieze, which covered the upper half of three walls in its side hall:
'Material: *Kaseinfarbe*, applied stucco, gilding. Decorative principle: respect for the layout of the hall; ornamented plaster surfaces. The three painted walls are in a continuous sequence. The first long wall opposite the entrance represents the longing for happiness, the suffering of weak mankind: the pleas they make to mankind to take up the struggle. The narrow wall: the enemy reinforces the giant Typhus, against whom even the gods have fought in vain; his daughters, the three gorgons, sickness, insanity, death. Lust and impurity, excess, gnawing grief. The longing and desires of mankind flying away over them. The second long wall: the longing for happiness is appeased by poetry. The arts lead us over to the ideal realm in which we can find only pure joy, pure happiness, pure love. A choir of angels in paradise.'

The conception of this *Gesamtkunstwerk* was taken one step further at the opening of the exhibition on 15 April 1902, when an arrangement of Beethoven's 9th Symphony for wind instruments, made by Mahler, resounded from the upper gallery of the Klimt-Hoffmann room. At once the significance of the exhibition in general, and of Klinger and Klimt's work in particular, was recognised, and moves were then made to preserve the frieze which Klimt had originally intended to be temporary.

After passing through several different hands the frieze came into possession of the Austrian state in 1973. Parts of it were in very bad condition, having been stored in garages and the like at some periods, but it underwent full restoration to modern standards for the *Dream and Reality* exhibition. Thus for the first time in 83 years, the public has been able to see this work in its entirety.

It was my belief that by far the most appropriate environment for displaying this work would be a reconstruction of that for which it was created, namely the Hoffmann room. Unfortunately it proved impossible to locate the decorative panels that originally occupied the wall niches, but thanks to support from the Vienna school of Applied Art, it was possible to reconstruct one of Hoffmann's sopraporta reliefs. From the art-historical point of view these are particularly important works, as the first abstract-constructive reliefs ever made, a decade and more before the idiom emerged elsewhere in the modernist avant-garde.

Precious little information remains to us on the room itself. There are absolutely no drawings, only the general plan which serves as a guide to the route through the original exhibition, printed in its catalogue and reproduced here. The original was simply a separate form inserted temporarily into the existing shell of the Secession building and constructed, as contemporaneous photos show, from temporary studwork. There are likewise relatively few verbal descriptions, and such as there are contain many inexactitudes and contradictions.

Our main source of information had to be such photographs of the XIV and XVIII Secessionist exhibitions as are held in the collection of the Austrian National Library or were available from various other sources.

Documentary photograph of the Hoffmann room for Klimt's Beethoven frieze at the Secession's spring exhibition of 1902; Klinger's 'Beethoven', *right*, and 'Mädchenkopf', *centre*.

All were in black-and-white, and none showed more than a limited portion of the room, but they did make it possible to reconstruct its appearance with considerable accuracy when augmented by information from other research.

The scale of different objects within the room was worked out from such clues as the known size of Klimt's frieze. We determined the exact nature and colour of the floor-covering by contacting the firm which had supplied the original carpet. We were able to piece together some of the colours from traces of paint that got onto Klimt's frieze panels when the walls were originally painted. Other colours were determined by a modern method which can determine colours in a black-and-white photograph if certain key elements are known, including the photographic emulsions originally exposed.

Further questions were resolved through an expert symposium held on 24 November 1984, which included Professor Eduard Sekler of Harvard University, and Drs Bisantz, Bogner and Hammer of the Austrian Ministry for the Preservation of Works of Art.

Analyses of the black-and-white photographs yielded the following information on colour: walls, beige; sopraportas reliefs, the same as the walls; carpet, a greyish light ochre. Shading was shown to have resulted not from a differentiation in the colour of the carpet itself, but from retouching of the photograph. Socles or plinths were discovered to have been a greyish light brown. Research undertaken by the Historical Museum of the City of Vienna confirmed that the floor was essentially grey, and likewise the plinths, which were of timber construction.

Written reports of the period differed in their descriptions of the wall colour. The newspaper *Wiener Allgemeine Zeitung* said the walls were 'white', Hevesi that they were 'yellowish'. Research by the Austrian Ministry for the Preservation of Works of Art determined that yellowish grey was the most likely colour.

Particular attention was paid to the materials used in the balcony of Hoffmann's room. Two things seemed to substantiate the theory that it was either gilded wood or wood painted a metallic colour. Firstly Hevesi described the skylight in the central hall as having a gilded frame. Secondly the lasts on the balcony rails were painted or gilded: this seems to rule out the possibility that they were encased in metal.

Only a tiny fragment of the back wall containing this balcony can be seen in photographs of the XIV Secessionist show. Photographs of the room in the XVIII show (when the room was devoted to Klimt) do not show much of the balcony either, although they indicate substantial changes to the interiors, which must also have affected the rear wall.

Of the buildings modelled to smaller scales, some, like Wagner's Church am Steinhof, had certainly also been modelled originally. This Church was one of several rendered in full colour (see page 19 below). Others, notably the two major houses by Hoffmann, were not rendered in the colours of the buildings themselves (see pages 34-35), but executed in the spirit of a 'new creation', in contrasting modelmaker's woods.

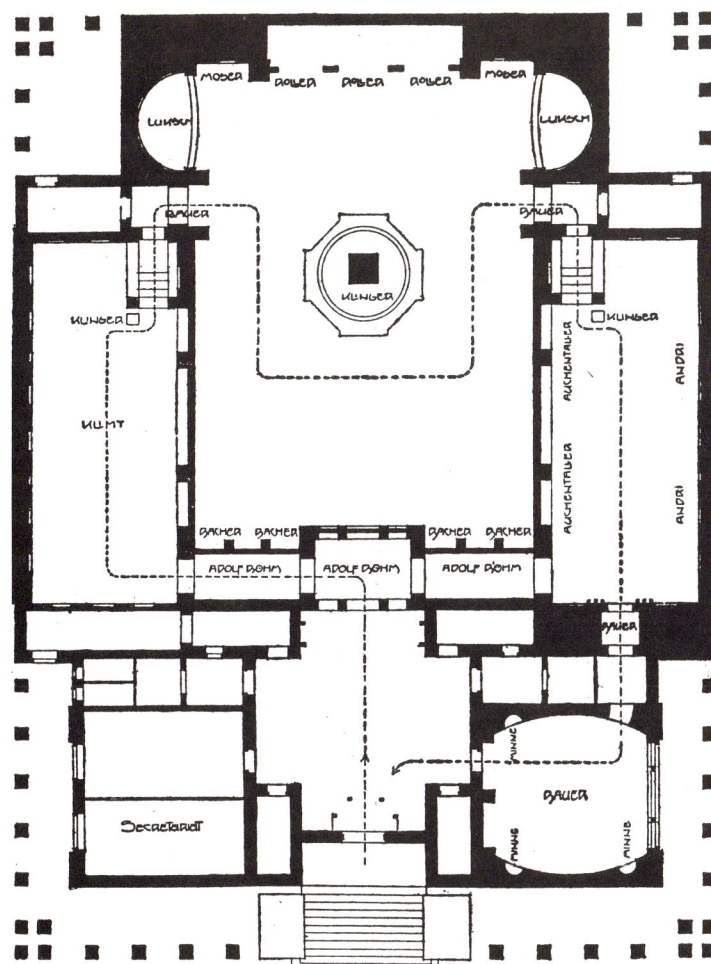
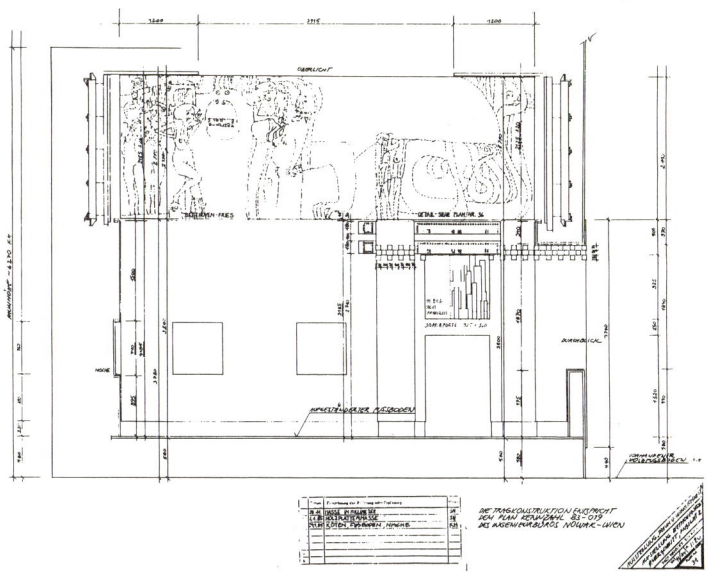

Above, plan of Olbrich's Secession building as laid out for the 1902 Beethoven show. **Right,** the Hoffmann-Klimt room under construction early 1902. **Upper right,** drawing by the Hollein office for 1985 reconstruction of the same end of the room. **Below,** documentary photograph of the original model of Wagner's Church am Steinhof, c 1905.

7

DESIGN FOR SALE: SHOPS OF THE WIENER WERKSTÄTTE

'The Wiener Werkstätte is the only organisation of artists and artistical workmen who from strictly original and constantly new ideas of their own design, build and furnish houses throughout as well as producing all articles in gold, silver, and all other metals, wood, leather, glass, china material etc.'
(English inscription on the corner of their Karlsbad shop, below.)

TODAY A HANDFUL OF THE DOMESTIC PRODUCTS designed by Secession members within their 'Vienna Art Workshops' remain in production by their original manufacturers. Thus glassware and furnishing fabrics by Hoffmann, in particular, may still be bought on Vienna's Kärntnerstrasse from the shops of Lobmeyr and Backhausen.[1] Production has been able to outlast the Werkstätte's own existence in these media because semi-mass production always required high-capital equipment beyond the means of craft workshops.

This situation in itself draws attention to an important difference between the Werkstätte and those English workshops, in particular Ashbee's Guild of Handicraft, which were the models when Hoffmann and Moser sought a means of realising their aspiration to offer 'complete design'. Amongst these Viennese there was far less of the socialist concern for the aesthetic and personal fulfillment of the workman, and a far greater concern with producing objects for the aesthetic satisfaction of the user. The products were certainly no less the result of commitment by the designer, but they had a real aspiration to be commercial.

With the currency of the 'lifestyle' concept of retailing today, it is easy to overlook the importance of the Wiener Werkstätte as perhaps the most important pioneer anywhere of that approach. The best account of its founding and early activity remains Peter Vergo's, which Eduard Sekler augments in some respects.[2] During the subsequent three decades of operation, from 1903 to 1932, it had three financial backers. When Fritz Wärndorfer, the first of the three, left Vienna relatively bankrupt in 1913 for the USA, the banker Otto Primavesi, already a Hoffmann client, stepped into his shoes and encouraged expansion. From 1926 until 1932, when commercial viability in a changed world proved unattainable, the backer was Primavesi's kinsman the textile magnate Kuno Grohmann. Beyond these basic facts the Werkstätte's history hitherto has been presented fragmentarily, as a dimension of its contributing designers' work, and even for its leading members, the literature remains remarkably incomplete. Still less documented, though noted in passing, are the changes of style and orientation resulting, for example, from Moser's departure in 1908, from Peche's new role in 1915 or Wimmer's dominance of the fashion and fabric side after that same date. There has been little exploration of the extent to which these design-retailers shaped or responded to the larger design climate, to market and design trends amongst their peers and competitors. To remain in commercial operation at all through those thirty volatile years was testament to remarkable design management, and it deserves recording as such.

Hollein's Künstlerhaus presentation of Werkstätte material in a 'shop' was an important reminder that what have become sanctified as 'artworks' in museums and salerooms were conceived and launched into the world as 'goods', albeit goods which proved again the unique potential of the plastic artist for achieving that synthesis of formal, material and functional coherence which is superlative design. Not finding in the extant literature any systematic list of the Werkstätte's shops and other premises, I thought it a useful means of focusing on that market interface, in the hope of stimulating deeper examination of this aspect of Secessionist activity.

Werkstätte designs reproduced here represent a range of media. Further Werkstätte products appear in colour on pages 36-45 below.

Catherine Cooke

1 J & L Lobmeyr, Kärntnerstr. 26; J Backhausen & Sohne, Kärntnerstr. 33.
2 P Vergo, *Art in Vienna 1898-1918*, 1975, pp.412-4.

- When registered by Hoffmann, Moser and Wärndorfer as a business on **19 May 1903**, the Werkstätte set up offices in Vienna IV, Heumühlgasse 6 (ref: ES p 62).
- In **October** that year it moved into a complex of offices, workshops for timber, leather, metalwork, and showrooms, converted for it by Hoffmann at Vienna VII, Neustiftgasse 32-4 (ES cat 81 and *Wien* p 287). Vergo p 134 quotes Moser on the programmatic 'colour-coding' of departments. Purkersdorf Sanatorium (Map Guide 1) was their first job of total design.
- **1906**, repertoire increased by formation of ceramics section under Dagobert/Peche, Michael Powolny and Bertold Löffler.
- **November 1907**, opened new main salerooms in Vienna's central shopping district at Graben 15, designed by Hoffmann (ES cat 116 and *Wien* p 286), built by Ast (cf Map Guide 73).
- **1908**, mosaics section created under Leopold Forstner; contributed particularly to the Steinhof and Lueger churches (Map Guide 8; 139) and Palais Stoclet.
- **1908**, opened a branch shop in Karlsbad (see illustration); striking Hoffmann design in 'white and grass green' (ES cat 126).
- **1912**, Neustiftgasse accommodation extended into Wagner's new building at nearby Döblergasse 4 (Map Guide 58).
- **1915**, fashion section formed under Peche and Mathilde Flögl (B&A p 55).
- **1916**, fashion shop opened in central Vienna at Kärntnerstrasse 41, designed by Hoffmann (ES cat 197 and B&A p 136) with Eduard Wimmer who was its artistic director. Another in Marienbad, largely fashions (ES cat 198).
- **About 1917**: shop opened in Zurich to designs by Peche (B&A p 136; graphics opposite).
- **1917-18**, textiles and lightfittings shop opened at Kärntnerstrasse 32 / Führichgasse, Hoffmann (ES cat 208).
- **1919**, opened shop in New York at 581 5th Avenue, run (? designed) by former Hagenbund leader Josef Urban (Vergo p 241; B&A p 137; *Wien* p 548 and Schm. p 340 give 1922).
- **1929**, shop opened in Berlin, site of earliest exhibition successes, at Friedrich Ebert Strasse 2-3, by Hoffmann with Haerdtl (ES cat 317, B&A p 136). Other provincial shops recorded at Breslau, Lucerne, Trieste.

Abbreviations: ES – Sekler *Hoffmann*; Wien – *Wien um 1900, Kunst und Kultur*, Brandstätter, Vienna, 1985; B&A – D Baroni & A d'Auria *Josef Hoffmann e la Wiener Werkstätte*, Milan 1981; Vergo – see footnote 2; Schm. – E Schmuttermeier 'Die Wiener Werkstätte' in *Traum und Wirklichkeit* catalogue, pp 336-340.

Werkstätte shop in Karlsbad, Hoffmann c 1908, from 1913 Werkbund Yearbook

Above, Peche label for Werkstätte fabrics, (courtesy Durant), 1916. **Top,** Löffler, wallpaper design, c 1915, and **inset**, Hoffmann, nightlight holder, c 1904; Powolny, china vase, c 1908, and Moser table lighter with ashtray and matchbox holder, 1904 (courtesy Mme Haas-Stoclet). **Left,** cutlery by Hoffmann for the Cabaret Fledermaus, c 1907.

'Hoffmann's cutlery is as carefully designed as the precision instruments of the scientist ... When it first appeared at the Secession exhibition, a tremor ran through the eating world. People claimed it was quite impossible to eat with it, not properly, not in the "English" manner! Herr Wärndorfer was the only person to buy it, but since then I have eaten with it myself, English as may be, and found it very practical.' (Hevesi, Altkunst-Neukunst, 1909)

ROBERT WAISSENBERGER
VIENNA — PAINTING AT THE TURN OF THE CENTURY

Gustav Klimt's poster for the first Secession exhibition, 1898 (Hist. Mus).

IN 1897 A REVOLT TOOK PLACE AMONGST THE ARTISTS OF Vienna, for in that year a new association of artists was formed calling itself the Secession. The revolutionary nature of this event derived from the fact that there had hitherto been only one artistic association in the city, a strictly traditional establishment which had its seat in the classical Künstlerhaus.

The Künstlerhaus, as organisation and exhibition centre, had its heyday in the 1860s and 70s. At that time it had attracted all the architects, sculptors and painters who had worked on aspects of the city's great Ringstrasse project, and had even managed to enlist as its President the great dictator of taste, and artistic colour-magician of the day, Hans Makart.

Gradually however another generation of artists had come to the fore, with different conceptions of art. They criticised the provinciality of art in Vienna, as well as the fact that even in art, commercial interests were paramount. They demanded that influences from abroad be allowed to penetrate the Viennese scene, that the Viennese establishment move into line with what was happening in the rest of the world.

After having been a major influence on Western European art for a decade, Art Nouveau thus came at last to Vienna where, as Jugendstil – the style of the young – it took on a form that was quite individual and specific to the city. The movement also came relatively late in terms of the age of many of the artists in Vienna who represented it, requiring them to undertake revolutionary changes in their behaviour and techniques. Jugendstil's two most important proponents, the architect Otto Wagner and the painter Gustav Klimt, were among those who had to undertake this major change of direction as more or less established practitioners. Klimt was already over thirty when first influenced by the new trends, and whilst not a product of the Makart school, he had worked in Makart's studio, and had thus already adopted the traditional modes.

The reputation and respect which Klimt holds today had its roots amongst his colleagues of that time. From the start he was ungrudgingly recognised by his fellow Secessionist artists as the most important of their group. In addition to being the leading light of the new association, he was its first formal President. The exhibitions which included his

Otto Wagner, Church for the North Austrian Mental Asylum 'am Steinhof, pen and watercolour perspectives by Wagner's office of the preliminary design, 1902 (Hist. Museum).

works were the real highpoints of the Secession's first years, but the fact that his pictures were frequently exhibited did not prevent them from being, amongst others, the cause of a great deal of opposition and outcry.

The first major scandal centred around his so-called 'Faculty Paintings', the representations of Medicine, Philosophy and Jurisprudence executed for the aula of Vienna University. These were allegorical compositions in which Klimt attempted to represent the themes underlying the various faculties in a totally unconventional manner. ('Medicine' is illustrated on page 15 below.) When those directly concerned with the paintings – the professors at the University – first saw them, they were literally speechless, and for a while no-one raised opposition to them. Slowly, however, a storm broke, and Klimt finally had to take his paintings back and forego the commission due to him. Yet when his critics were asked exactly what they thought a represent-

ation of the faculties of the University should look like, they could only suggest a series of portraits of great personalities who had made major contributions to their particular fields of study. Thus the Faculty Paintings never reached their intended destintation.

Another cause of much argument was Klimt's 'Beethoven Frieze', shown at the Fourteenth Secession Exhibition of 1902. Many visitors deemed the work too free, too challenging, and even obscene, but the frieze and the exhibition of which it formed an integral part were together one of the most important manifestations of the new style in Vienna. It is therefore fitting that the 'Beethoven Frieze', restored and on show again for the first time in eighty years, should have been one of the focal points of the *Dream and Reality* exhibition.

The Jugendstil gradually spread throughout Vienna, and another new artistic association called the Hagenbund, progressive though of somewhat different philosophy, was formed in 1900. Like the Secession

Gustav Klimt, 'Pallas Athene', 1898, in the frame of Klimt's design (Hist. Museum). See also page 50.

a few years previously, it established its own exhibition gallery in the city. But it was Klimt and his circle who gave the Jugendstil its distinctive character. Rejecting the indulgently free-curved, floral motifs characteristic of Art Nouveau elsewhere, they created a language of clear, geometrical forms that was to be the pinnacle of the Viennese Jugendstil achievement.

The change in Gustav Klimt's painting which lead to the creation of his own unique style came around 1902. He was a man who absorbed many different influences from the art of Europe and beyond, and adapted them to his own purposes. Byzantine painting, for example, was a major influence, but so too was the art of Eastern Asia and Greek Antiquity. A man highly aware of the evolution within his own work, he is nonetheless best known today for the paintings of his 'high Secessionist' period with their rich, gold-ornamented surfaces – in particular for 'The Kiss' of 1901-2, and his 'Portrait of Adele Bloch-Bauer' of 1907 (see pages 55 and 51/53 below).

By 1908 these leaders of the Secession found the Secession itself becoming an establishment, and with their shows of 1908 and 1909 the 'Klimt group' broke away to present their work in a special new complex of galleries built for them by architect member Josef Hoffmann, under the simple name of Kunstschau – the Art Show. These Kunstschauen provided the opportunity for the initial, radical Secessionists to sum up what they had achieved and to show their particular brand of late Art Nouveau as a movement and school distinct from what had happened elsewhere.

Time was not standing still, however, and there was no resting on their laurels. Those who visited the Kunstschauen of 1908 and 1909 expecting to see the same art they had now got used to, however reluctantly, were disappointed. For these exhibitions provided the platforms for two young artists of the next generation to launch

Egon Schiele, 'Self portrait with spread fingers', 1911 (Hist. Museum).

something new again. Here it was Oskar Kokoschka and Egon Schiele who, despite the support of the established members of the group, created scandals.

Kokoschka encountered great opposition at the 1908 Kunstshau, being dubbed by Ludwig Hevesi – a critic otherwise very favourably disposed towards the group – as 'the chief tearaway' (der Oberwildling). His pictures were indeed something new, absolutely without that aestheticism of Klimt's work, especially that of his 'Golden' period. Kokoschka broke new ground with a brutal, direct use of materials, with his attempt to nail the psyche of his subject, in particular of his portraits, far more directly than any of his predecessors. These works represented the phase in Kokoschka's work which has subsequently been most highly regarded.

The next year, 1909, it was Schiele's turn. Here another young artist showed his movement away from Jugendstil philosophies to a highly personal view of art and to a new expressionism. Like Kokoschka, Schiele concerned himself with representations of people, but his methods were entirely different. His subject was man's tragic situation. All his works show the dependency of human existence upon fate, communicating this theme in a manner unlike anyone before him.

Towards the end of the first decade of the century, there was a clear change in the direction of painting, even if it was not universally recognised. Two men more or less on the fringe of the painterly community – Richard Gerstl and his friend Arnold Schonberg – were paving the way directly into an art perhaps more characteristic of the new century than the belated Art Nouveau had been. Schonberg's visionary pictures have tended to be overshadowed by his musical compositions, and Gerstl's inspired landscapes and expressive portraits have remained in very unjustified obscurity.

Around these leading figures were of course a whole pleiad. Some

Left, Richard Gerstl, 'Self-portrait', c 1905, and **above,** Egon Schiele, 'My room, Neulengbach', 1911. (Both Hist. Museum. All pictures and page 3, © Direktion der Museen der Stadt Wien)

like Klimt were the centre of a group; Schiele, Kokoschka and Gerstl were individuals who had no following at the time in the wider community though highly esteemed by their close colleagues. The totality, however, was a period of painterly achievement which established Vienna as a world leader in its time.

Hofrat Dr Robert Waissenberger is Director of the Historical Museum of the City of Vienna, and with Professor Hans Hollein was the principal creator of the Dream and Reality *exhibition.*

DREAM AND REALITY
VIENNA 1890-1930
INSTALLATION IN THE KÜNSTLERHAUS VIENNA
DESIGNED BY HANS HOLLEIN
COMMENTARY BY CATHERINE COOKE

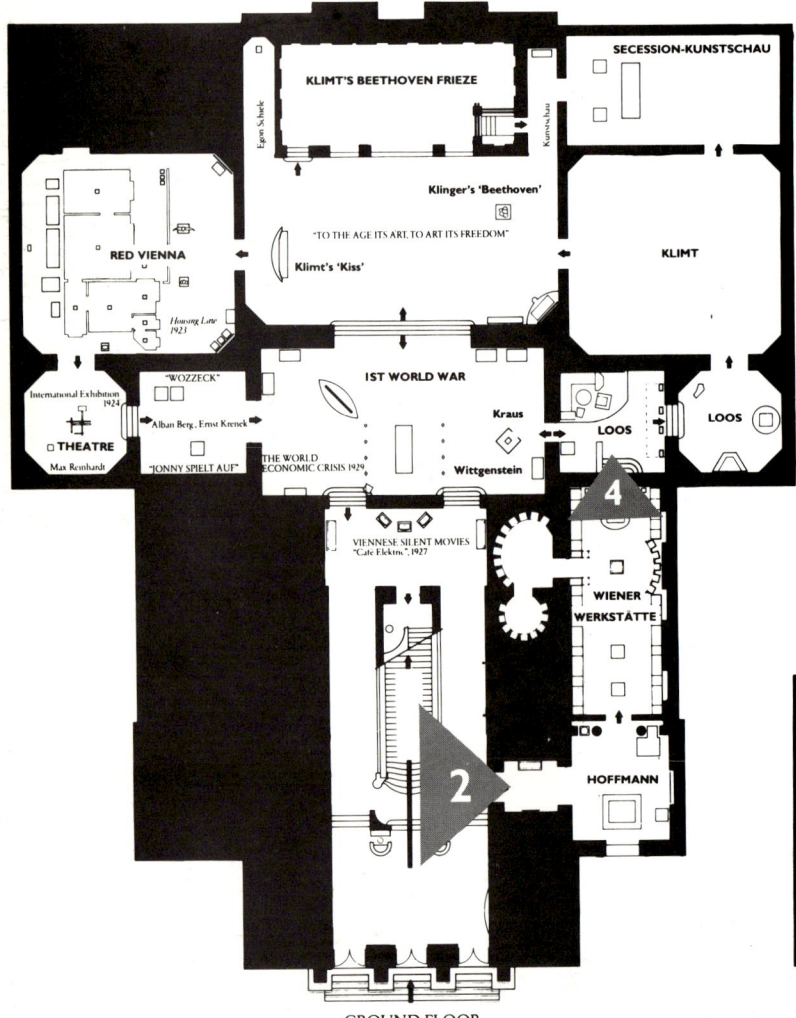

PLAN OF THE EXHIBITION

AGGRANDISEMENT IN THE 1870s MAKART STRAUSS
& THE STOCKMARKET CRASH

THE ARTISTIC AND POLITICAL EVENTS recounted in the Dream and Reality show were dramatic. From the point of view of the arts (and by that word I necessarily include architecture), the choice of location had a frisson which it requires a certain historical knowledge to understand. Vienna's Künstlerhaus was not literally an Academy, but by the late 1890s its monopoly of influence gave it just that kind of establishment role, at the heart of the great patronage market which the Austro-Hungarian Empire still represented. It was thus precisely from this building, and from the cliques who showed and politicked here, that the Secessionists seceded.

Hans Makart, painter of ebullient histories, was its President. In 1879 he designed a great street pageant in which Vienna's haut-bourgeois depicted themselves and their city's glories with maximum narcissism. They had just hosted a World Exhibition. They congratulated themselves on the genius they enjoyed in *Die Fledermaus*. And they hoped its music would continue to drown the tremours of the Stock Market collapsing under them.

For adherents of Secessionist fresh-air, the welcome parade of Makart's burgers, **opposite**, was the greeting of a host just a little too glad to see one. Hung amidst Herr President's own paintings on the top landing were some flatteringly similar works by a young pupil in his studio named G Klimt; the time-bomb was ticking away.

The sequence of 'chapters' by which the exhibition proceeded was not perfectly chronological. It was rather a synthesis of the building form with dramatic visual story-telling in light and colour. In selecting and presenting the photographic sequence that follows, I have tried not just to document the elements of the installation, but to preserve some of those moments of shock and constrast on the page.

Left: installation plans of first floor, ground floor and basement, Künstlerhaus, Vienna. **Preceding page**: Klimt's 'Medicine', 1900-7, and its nude modelled as the symbol of 'Dream' on the Künstlerhaus roof opposite Reality' derived from the Karl Marx Hof development of 1926. (Photos *left* by Erich Pedevilla, *right* by Georg Riha.)

OTTO WAGNER ARCHITECTURE

Climax of the ascent through Makart's heavy and claustrophobic historicism, and a release from its social introversion, was the blazing white and gold of the new model of Wagner's Church am Steinhof of 1904-7 **(opposite)**, spotlit, on axis, on a pedestal, and approached from below as on the real hillside. It is seen again in the transverse view of the Wagner room, **below**. Turning point for the route, it was equally a focal statement for the whole first floor of the show. As church of a mental hospital, the building was not just a masterpiece in the Secessionist synthesis of art and architecture, but an embodiment of the synthesis between those arts and the ideas of inter-personal analysis and manipulation underlying the political and psychological themes also presented on that floor. **Right:** the church today. **Below:** the model, drawings and interior views of the church as Baroque focus to the greyer Rationalism also modelled in three dimensions at each end, and the Wagner drawings of all periods around the walls.

Illuminated interior views of the Church and of Wagner's contemporaneous Post Office Savings Bank reinforced Hollein's juxtaposition of the Baroque and Rationalist themes. The selection of drawings stressed that genuine embracing of modern technology which gave such unusually solid foundations and conviction to Wagner's stylistic Rationalism. Both communications and transportation were central and recurrent themes of his oeuvre, and prominently represented here through the *Die Zeit* telegraph agency, as well as the Post Office, the Stadtbahn city railway network, his contributions to the Danube Canal, and his pioneering urban and regional planning work for Vienna's future.

Right: Post Office Savings Bank building, 1904-6, main entrance view of the new model.

Function made decorative: the Post Office Savings Bank, Georg Coch Platz, Vienna, 1904-6: interior of the main hall specially cleared of its recently remodelled furniture and planters for photography. Wagner's original cubic stools are used here, and most of his special furniture and fittings remain elsewhere in the building, though the heating system no longer operates through his cylindrical 'columns'.

Baroque made functional: the Catholic Church of St Leopold in the Vienna City Mental Hospital at Steinhof, 1905-7: recent view of the interior, where the exigencies of its peculiar function determined many of the details, as well as its sunny mood. Male and female patients had to enter separately: pews are short (4 persons) and widely spaced for extracting any who cause disturbance; strong warm-air heating is incorporated into nave pillars; surfaces are non-disfigurable as well as hygenic, and a slightly sloped floor allows swilling out as well as enhanced views from all pews.

Entrance hall to Wagner's 1912 competition project for an Emperor Franz Josef Municipal Museum on the Smeltz: one of the richest examples of his late style, where Baroque and Rationalist dimensions of the earlier work are synthesised to enhance awareness of the space and of the vigorous modern construction. The dualism is played upon in his own juxtaposition of conspicuous telephone facilities to the Donner-Brunner sculptures, masterpieces of the Viennese Baroque.

Like the battle to show what a modern hotel could be, with his projects for the Ringstrasse of 1910 and for Karlsplatz during the next year, the sequence of Wagner's proposals for a Kaiser Franz Josef Museum, first on his own initiative and then in the relocated competition, were given prominence by Hollein as examples of Wagner's energetic interventions to influence – albeit unsuccessfully – the conservative trend of current debates on Vienna's development.

Opposite: full-size reconstuction of the dorway to Wagner's offices for *Die Zeit's* telegraph bureau at Kärntnerstrasse 39, built in 1902 and destroyed in 1908.

When Carl Moll got the Kunstrat (Art Council) to agree his proposal of 1899 for a special gallery of 'modern art', itself a controversial idea in the conservative art fraternity, Wagner, as an active Kunstrat member, seized another opportunity to press his idea for a major gallery on the Ringstrasse and in 1900 presented this unsolicited scheme for 'A gallery of the art of our time'. Its elevation onto Vordere Zollamstrasse, **above,** was the only 'finished' part. In his typically 'organic' conception, each decade of the new century would decorate its own room as it installed its work.

The hanging of Wagner's work by theme rather than date made many enlightening juxtapositions. Here formal and compositional constants run through from the soft early work with its characteristically Secessionist floral themes, to his highly personal late style seen in the hard ceramics of the Kaiserbad Dam control building for the Danube Canal of 1906-7, built to control flooding on the main river.

Opposite: Wagner as city planner. A view towards St Stephen's Cathedral showing various proposed facilities of the Danube Canal embankments with two new bridges, 1897: *top right,* his first scheme for the Ferdinandsbrücke, and in the *foreground* the Aspernbrücke to carry the Ringstrasse. The drawing in its cartouche was part of a folio presented to Emperor Franz Josef for his jubilee by the Academy of Fine Arts in 1898.

Reinhold Völkel, 'In the Cafe Griensteidl', 1896

Richard Neutra, who grew up in Wagner's Vienna, recalled in a memoir of 1969: 'I already knew as a child that he had the ability to win friends in widely different camps, from Lueger to Lux: the first a great mayor and the highly original popular leader of a great party which he himself had created, the second a faithful publicist – for Lueger's opposition – and also ... Wagner's first biographer.' The indispensibility of such political relationships to the achievement of city planning ideas was reflected in the hanging here by direct juxtaposition of Wagner's planning schemes with the Karl Lueger material in the next room **(opposite, top)**.

Lueger's energy and the extent of the administrative reform he promised are indicated by the Emperor Franz Josef's two-year prevarication over ratifying his electon to Burgermeister in 1895. He eventually held office from 1897 to 1910. In a city where all public utilities including energy and transport were still in the hands of capitalists (many British), he introduced massive municipalisation that made possible integrated realisation of such projects as Wagner's Stadtbahn – initially conceived under Vienna's 1892 Transport Act – and the green-belt immediately accessible at the end-station of every street-car line.

Lueger room, **opposite top:** Materials on the municipalisation of Vienna's gas and street-car networks, on its electricity and water supplies, and on Lueger's Christian-Democratic social policy, hung amidst scenes from Imperial and Municipal balls in the sugary realism of Wilhelm Gause. The city banner and throne for Lueger, *left,* are by Wagner (1908 & 1904). The sequence of 'chapters' moves, *right,* into opera, where the unalloyed dreaming of Strauss' era on the landing is quenched by a cold shower of musical and visual reality under Mahler.

The anti-semitism of which Lueger himself was a prominent spokesman prevented Gustav Mahler, too, from achieving the top job in his field until 1897, when baptism into Roman Catholicism facilitated his appointment as Director of the Vienna Court Opera. His decade there was amongst its finest, for musical integrity, and for coherence of aural and visual intergration resulting from his collaboration with Alfred Roller as stage designer – the artist who in 1898 did *Ver Sacrum's* first cover.

In this room, **opposite middle,** Mahler presides in a bust by Rodin and a frieze derived from Otto Böhler's contemporary caricatures. The main focus is on the sensation-creating 1903 Mahler-Roller production of Wagner's *Tristan and Isolde,* where realistic acting combined with Roller's designs to create a new definition of opera as Gesamtkunstwerk.

Closing the view, on the threshold between this dream and the next, sharper, political reality, stood a full-size replica of Josef Hoffmann's tombstone for Mahler, who died in 1911. Beyond it, the pink and purple of dream became blazing scarlet and the frieze a standardised procession of red flags. A statue of Lueger's fierce opponent the socialist Franz Schuhmeier – naturalism from his tomb juxtaposed with the Secessionist abstraction – stood amidst trade union banners. Here as in various other sections a video brought the history to life. Dominating the literary documents were 25 years of propaganda pamphlets, and manifestos of the Austrian Social-Democratic Workers' Party **(opposite, bottom)**, from 1889 when Victor Adler unified them, through to the outbreak of War in 1914.

The next 'chapter' **(pages 28-9)** was a forcefully three-dimensional reminder of the physical environment in which these ideas were fought out. An entire room with natural light and windows onto the Karlsplatz was filled by the five-meter-square model of Vienna within the Ringstrasse, made in 1897-8, from the city's Historical Museum. Semper's notions of an Imperial Forum were never completed, but the Ringstrasse conception gave shape to the city as focus of the 54-million strong Austro-Hungarian Empire. Ten years after the model, in 1908, Vienna was the world's fifth largest metropolis after London, New York, Paris and Berlin, with all the associated inequities dividing state and mercantile architecture from slums. Learning from Haussman's Paris, the Ringstrasse was created from 1857 onwards by demolition of the city's medieval walls and ravelins rather than private property. The sequence of grandly historicist public buildings erected on it are listed in the Map Guide.

From this complancent environment of mahogany and gold the extraordinary blue light with which Hollein evoked the world of Freud was one of his most powerful and most elegantly economical spaces **(pages 30-1)**. It was the better, perhaps, for being forced into immateriality by London's refusal to lend the great man's original consulting room furniture.

When a holographic representation was prohibited, Hollein conceived a tiny symbolic model of the couch and Freud's chair, swathed in a sinister backlight on a corner pedestal, as focus of a room which celebrates the 1899 *Interpretation of Dreams* more chillingly, for the absence in it of any real objects. All dematerialised by the hypnotic blue light were documents on the anti-Freudian controversy, in particular on the young Otto Weininger's latently anti-semitic and anti-feminist *Inheritance and Character* of 1903; paintings by Alfred Kubin that represented Freud's influence on Symbolism, and a black-and-white reproduction of Klimt's now destroyed ceiling painting for the University of 1900-7, representing *Medicine,* whose nude figure was model for the gilded symbol of 'Dream' on the Künstlerhaus roof directly above.

POLITICS ' PLANNING & PSYCHOLOGY

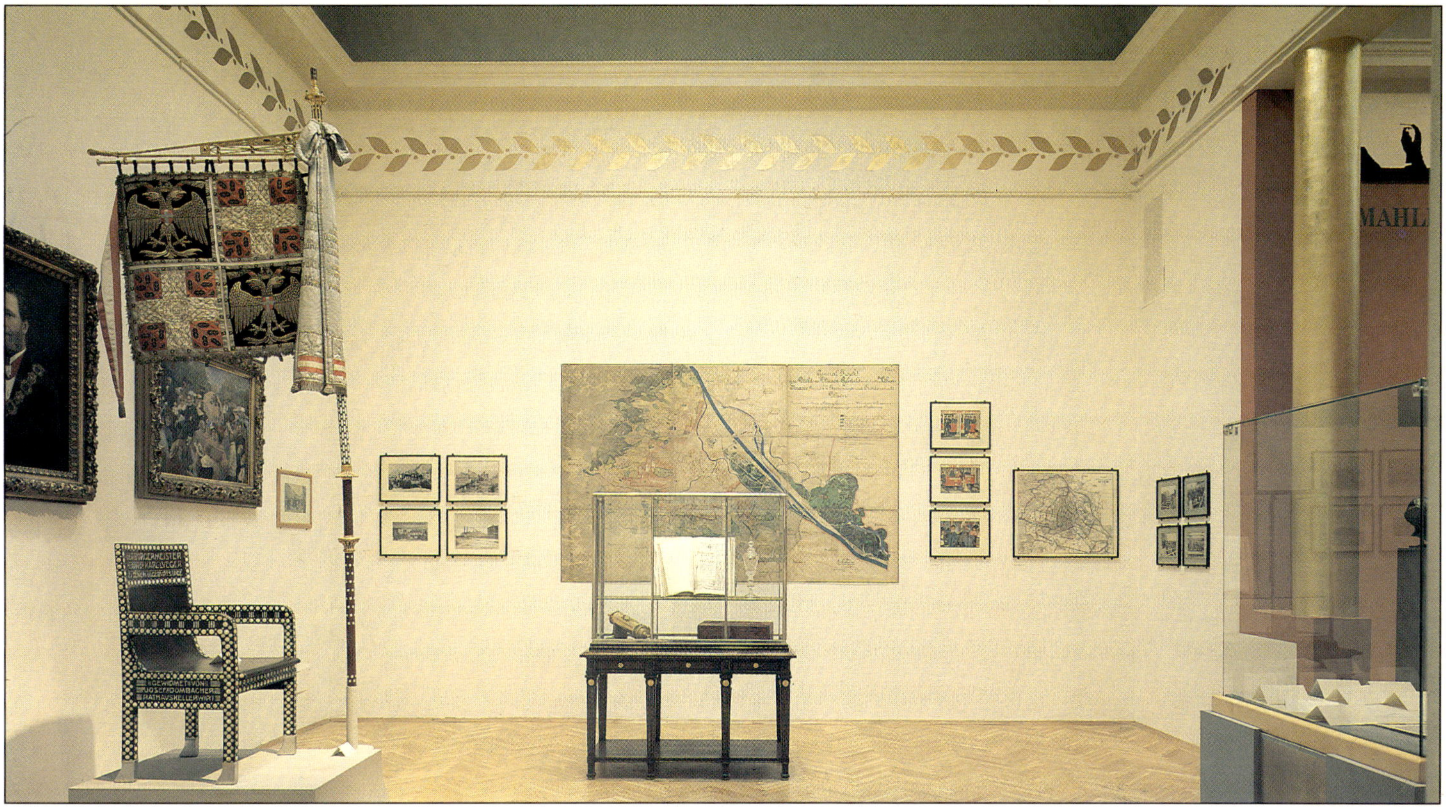

Tristan und Isolde

MARZ 1912
MARZ 1913

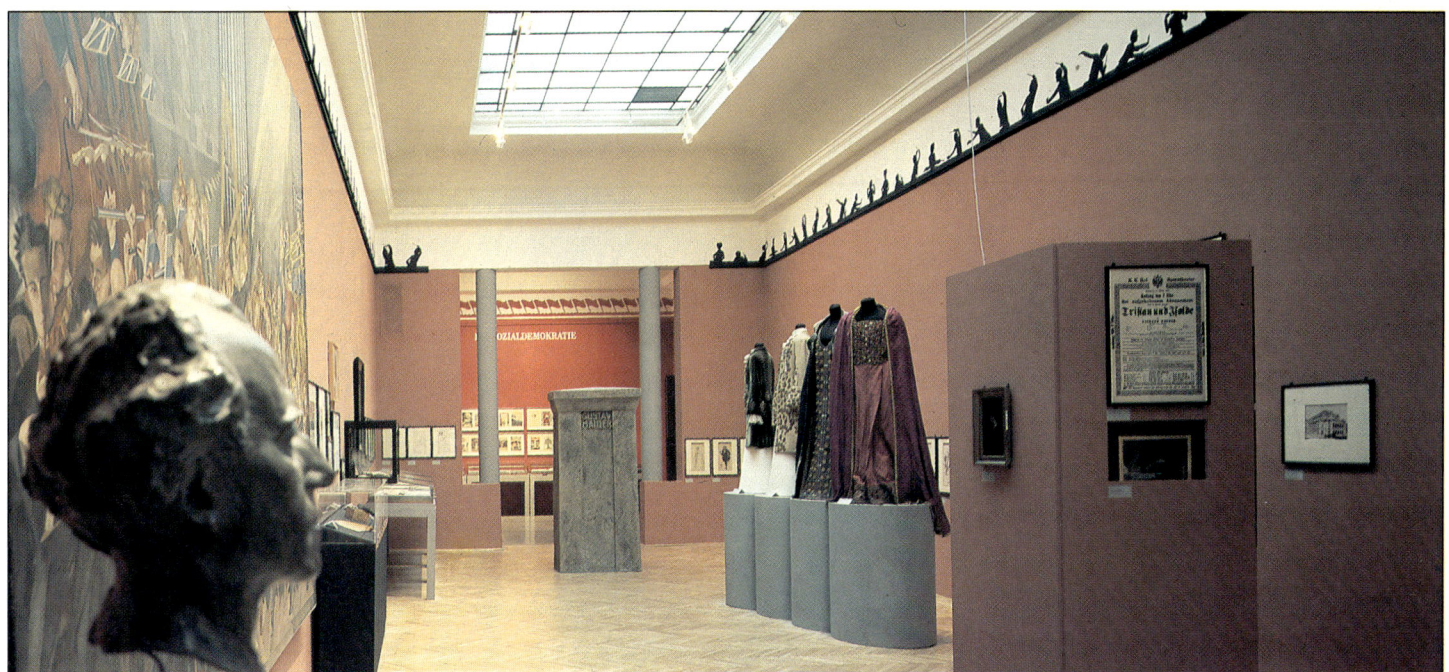

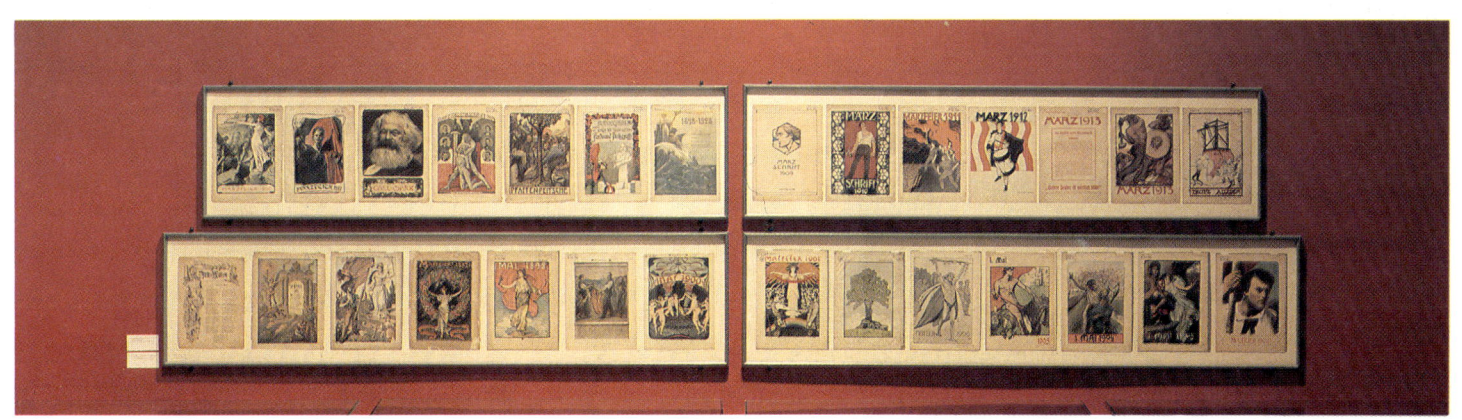

Sigmund Freud's armchair and couch in his consulting room (documentary photograph).

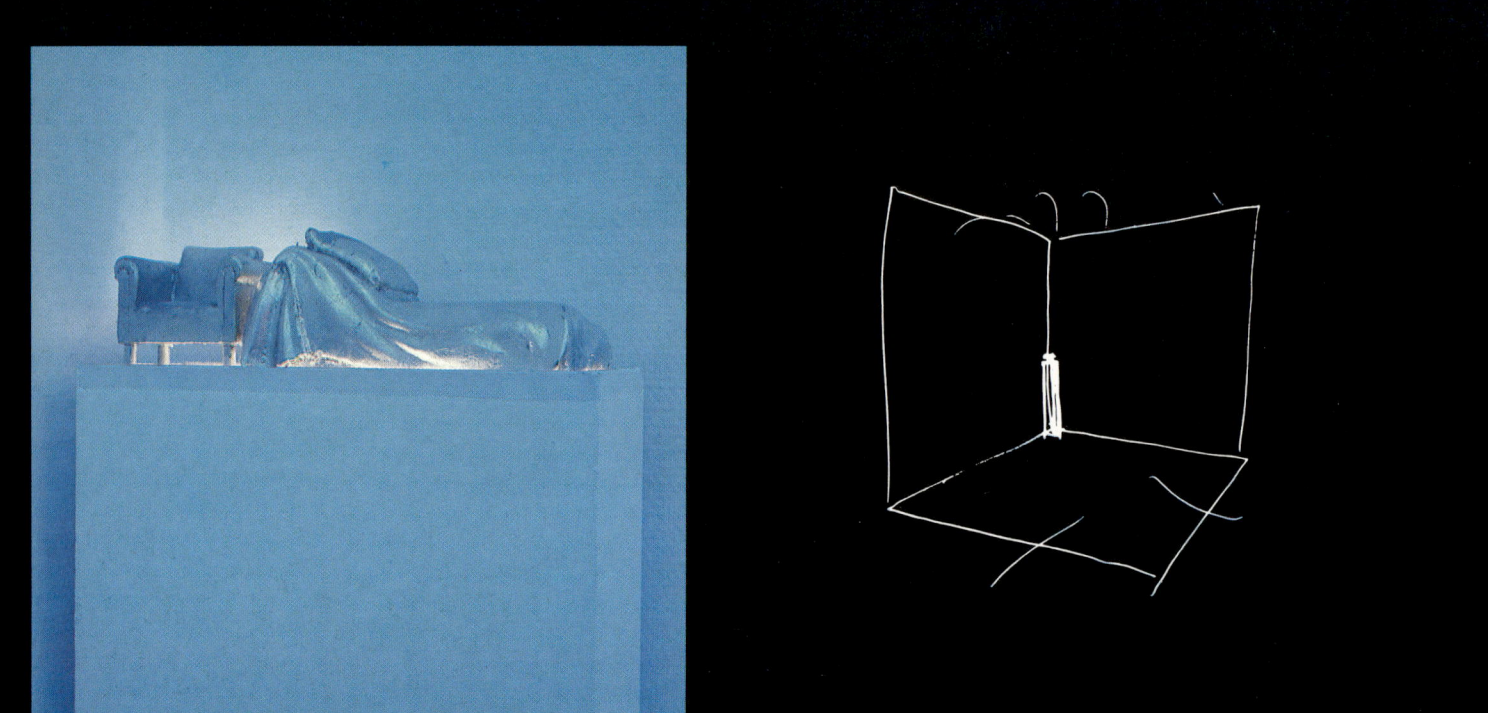

Opposite, far left: close-up of the chair and couch model on its pedestal, and **left:** Hollein's sketch for the model's placement in the room. **Above:** his sketch for the model, and the Freud room, a near-cube with crazy-patterned floor and blue light evoking *The Interpretation of Dreams (Die Traumdeutung)*. The reproduction of Klimt's *Medicine* hangs out of view in the extreme top right foreground (see pages 15 & 26 above). Colour photographs by Zugmann

LITERARY LIFE

The blue light of Freud is never wholly out-of-sight down the entire left side of the first floor. Pink posters in the space adjoining his are part of the 'chapter' on the Jewish question in Austria from Herzl's *Jewish State* of 1896 through to 1930.

In the sunnier main gallery Richard Gerstl's 1905 portrait of Arnold Schönberg surveys another generation of Vienna's musical avant-garde: himself, Alban Berg and Anton Webern, with his own paintings and records of his friendship with Kokoschka.

More influenced by Freud is the literary circle of 'Young Vienna' in the foreground, propagators of an aesthetic rooted in powerful use of the psychological detail. The bohemian physical environment of Karl Kraus, Arthur Schnitzler, von Hofmannsthal and the Secessionists' great champion Hermann Bahr is evoked by interiors of the cafés where they congregated and *left*, by a reconstructed corner of the Graben Hotel room which was home to Adolf Loos' friend Peter Altenberg on the eve of War in 1914. *Left top:* documentary photo of another corner of Altenberg's room.

Above: Hoffmann room. **Below:** model of the Skywa-Primavesi House, 1913-15, garden side.

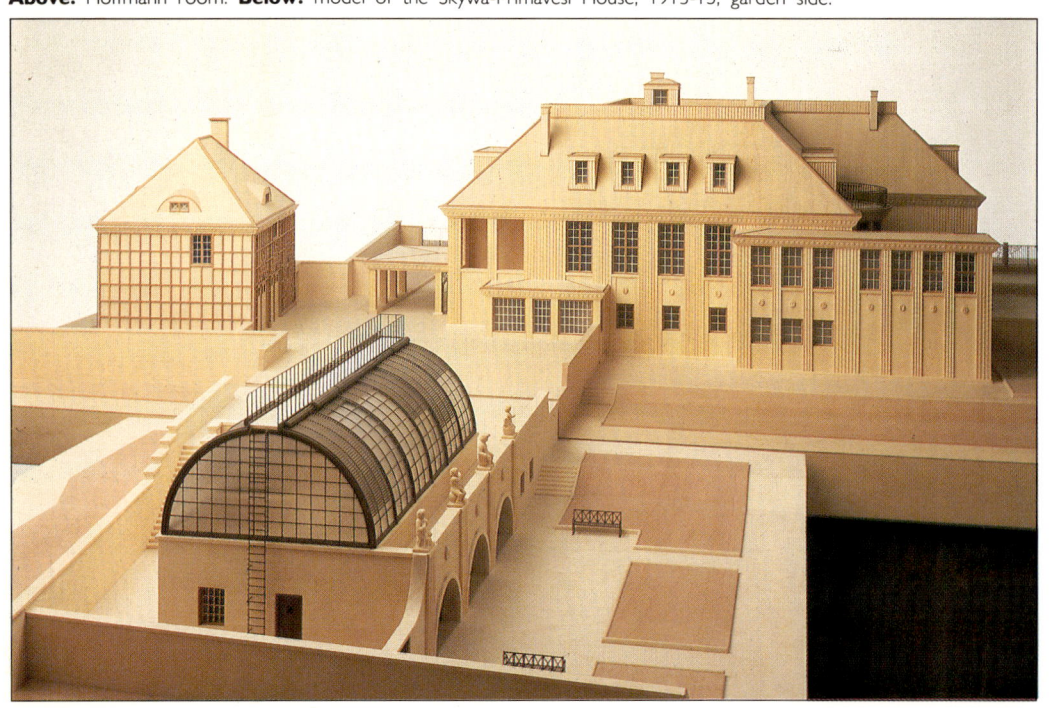

JOSEF HOFF MANN

ARCHITECTURE

Warm greys and clear volumes in the Hoffmann room. The carpet is his design for the 1911/12 Austrian Arts & Crafts exhibition. New models of Primavesi *(left)* and Stoclet Houses flank Moll's 1903 view of the terrace in his Hoffmann house (see Map Guide nos. 19 & 75).

Model of the Stoclet House, Brussels, 1906-11, **above:** street view, **below:** garden side.

WIENER WERK STÄTTE

Moving from Hoffmann's architecture into the Wiener Werkstätte 'shop', **opposite,** warm grey becomes cool blue. This main display room of Werkstätte design was one of the show's most dramatic and attractive spaces. Hollein's design draws on several direct formal sources in Hoffmann. The narrow space with free-standing central items recalls his WW shop of 1907 at Graben 15; the high-pitched section, the fabric shop at Kärntnerstrasse 32 of 1917, though the use of draped fabric owes more to his 12th Secession show of 1901. He used the carpet again in their fashion department at Kärntnerstr. 41 in 1916. The display system in the vitrines was an earlier design by Hollein for shop-fitting, and his insistence on lighting from within the vitrines presented the items as 'retail goods' with great historical authenticity.

Left: vases by Moser and pupils; *centre*: table lamp by Hoffmann; *right*: silver by both, also Peche and Czeschka.

Clothes by Blauensteiner, Moser, Zovetti; fans — Löffler, Peche, Czeschka; umbrella — Hoffmann. Display cabinet by Hoffmann for Stoclet.

Centre: Hoffmann table 1903-4; coffee service 1910; and cutlery for Wärndorfer. Fashion picture display in style of his WW room at the 1914 Werkbund show, Cologne.

Inset: Werkstätte designs from the Stoclet collection, Brussels.

Hollein's display system of felt-covered 'pedestals' on perforated steel panels. Silverware – mainly Moser and Hoffmann.

Left to right: Hoffmann champagne flute painted by Reni Schschl, c 1920; Hoffmann bowls in *messing martelé*, c 1905; three Moser vases of 1900. (Courtesy Mme Haas-Stoclet).

Centre: ceramic Cupid by Löffler, 1912, and Hoffmann's original carpet. *Right:* coffee set by Sika, 1901-2.

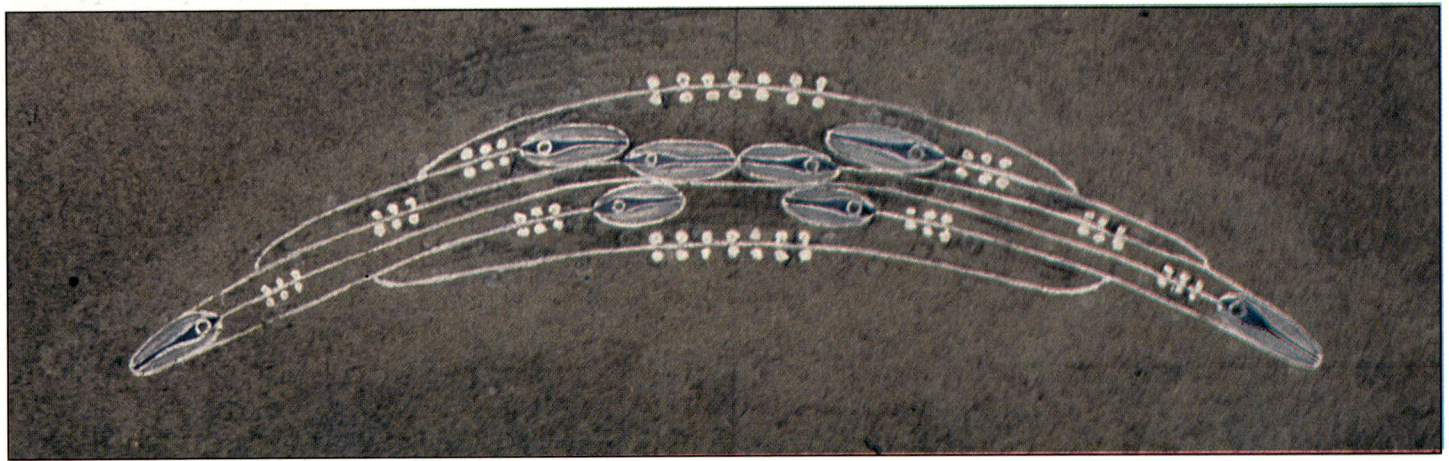

Wiener Werkstätte jewelry, glassware and graphics displayed in intimate *cabinets* off the main 'shop'.

Opposite, *top:* the display of Werkstätte jewelry, including designs by Otto Prutscher, Dagobert Peche, Bernard Löffler, Eduard Josef Wimmer-Wisgrill, Georg Klimt and Carl Otto Czeschka as well as Moser and Hoffmann, all made in the Werkstätte workshops.
Middle: Brooch, 1908, in silver and semi-precious stones, and belt-fastening of c.1907, in gilded copper and enamel, both to designs by Hoffmann.
Bottom: design by Kolo Moser inscribed by himself as being for 'simple diadem of silver, pearls, enamel, mother of pearl and greenstone', c.1900.
This page, above: the glassware display with items by Moser, Hoffmann, Jutta Sika, Josef Olbrich, Otto Prutscher, Hilda Jesser, Dagobert Peche, Julius Zimpel. Most were manufactured by E.Bakolovits & Son, though Hoffmann's was by J & L.Lobmeyr, who still have some items in production, and others in the museum at their shop on Kärntnerstrasse, or by Ludwig Moser & Son in Karlsbad.
Right: woven furnishing fabric by Hoffmann entitled 'Desire', 1904, recently brought back into production by the original manufacturers, J.Backhausen & Son, whose shop is also on Kärntnerstrasse.
Below: design by Moser, n.d., for the endpapers of a book.

Werkstätte postcards: **top left,** attributed to Hoppe, depicts the entrance to Hoffmann's temporary exhibition buildings of 1908 for the Kunstschau, on site of today's Konzerthaus. *Others, l-r,* by Divéky, Marisch, Nechansky, Löffler, Divéky. **Below:** ladies shoes, size 39, from the WW c.1914.

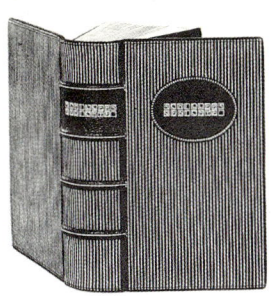

Above: Tooled leather goods executed by the Wiener Werkstätte's own craftsmen: a book binding in red and gold designed by Kolo Moser, 1905; a man's briefcase in black and gold of unknown designer; a ladies handbag by Josef Hoffmann for the Werkstätte fashion shops in green and gold, of about 1916.
Right: cupboard doors from Hoffmann's remodellling of Max Biach's apartment, 1902, in blue and white he used widely for furniture. The stained glass design has been attributed to Moser, was reproduced as a silk scarf by Artfoulard amongst souveniers for the Exhibition.

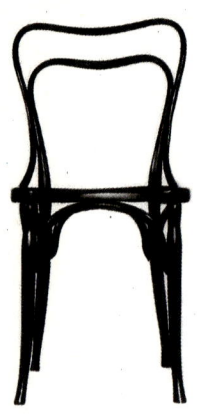

Loos, 1899: Chair in cane and bentwood, table of bentwood, marble and brass, for the Cafe Museum, manufactured by J & J Kohn.

Furniture was displayed against the plain white and grey in one big room which, as Hoffmann described his main space of the XII Secession show in November 1901, was 'covered like a tent with white fabric'.

Below, *centre:* Writing desk and chair of inlaid ebony and beech made for the mother of WW financier Fritz Wärndorfer, 1903-4; *behind it, left:* Hoffmann sewing table (see below); standing clock by Loos, 1909-11; girl's bedroom furniture in blue & white, Hoffmann, 1902; painting by Moll of his wife and child in their Hoffmann house, 1903; *right:* Moser's black-and-white chair, 1903, for the XVIII Secession show that year, devoted to Klimt; glazed bookcase and low cupboard by Wimmer Wisgrill.

Hoffmann, c.1901: Upholstered chair in black lacquered wood with aluminium feet, made by J & J Kohn.

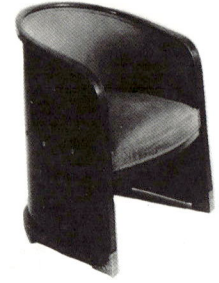

Hoffmann, 1901-2: Upholstered armchair in mahogany-faced ply and beech with aluminium fastenings and trim, made by Kohn.

Hoffmann, 1929-30: Armchair of beech, painted red, for the 1930 Werkbund exhibition in Vienna.

Below, *centre*: dining room, by Moser, 1900, in maple and marquetry with brass fittings, made by Portois & Fix, exhibited, with the buffet, *left*, at the VII Secession show in that year. *Left to right* behind: the Flöge showcase (see below); white girl's bedroom furniture by Hoffmann, 1902, for Max Biach's apartment in Mayahofgasse; his hexagonal table (see below); painting by Carl Moll of his wife Anna at her writing desk in their Hoffmann house, c.1910; Hoffmann's 'Sitting machine' of 1905 and red Werkbund chair (see below) both partially concealed behind the doll's house by Magda von Moutner-Markhof of 1908, displayed in the 'art for children' section of that year's Kunstschau; in niche, Wagner's boardroom furniture for the Saving Bank, 1904-6, made by Thonet. (Colour photographs by Zugmann.)

Hoffmann, 1902:
Hanging lamp in white metal and coloured glass for the Biach apartment.

Hoffmann, 1905:
Hanging lamp in copper made by WW for refurnishing of Hermann Wittgenstein's flat on Salesianergasse.

Moser, 1904:
Showcase in black-stained maple, glass and white metal, from the reception room of the Flöge sisters' fashion house in Mariahilferstrasse.

Hoffmann, 1904:
Hexagonal table in black-stained maple and white marble, made by WW.

Hoffmann, 1903-4:
Table of stained maple with white metal trims, also made with flaps and pouch as a sewing-table.

AD: LOOS
OLF

The Loos room at one end of the Werkstätte section **(above)** is an interesting comparison with the Hoffmann room at the other end (page 34), in both its initial selection and its treatment. Even its minimally classical delineation is played down, where the stronger architectural ordering of the Hoffmann space was heightened. The result is an unornamented space of white in which the only emphasis and appeal to visual sensibility is the patterned marble, of the *Chicago Tribune* model's pedestal, *left,* and the plinth of the Loos-building model, *centre,* which concentrate attention on that feature of the building's elevation in both exterior models and the structural one, *right* and **opposite.**

All three were new models. *Behind* hang elevations and plans of the two projects, the so-called Loos-building or 'Building on Michaelerplatz' of 1909-11, with premises for the mens outfitters Goldman & Salatsch on the two lower floors and residential accommodation above, and Loos's 31-storied entry for the *Chicago Tribune* building competition of 1922, the so-called '*Chicago Tribune* Column'. *Right,* Kokoschka's 1909 study of one Goldman child with hands of the others, and *below it,* period photographs of Loos' first shop interiors for the firm at Graben 20, executed 1898-1903 and since destroyed.

Above the central model hangs the poster for Loos' public defence of the Michaelerplatz building on 11 December 1911. The 'motto' – 'This monster of a building' referred to the attack by a municipal councillor, on Rykl, in October the previous year. When two thousand people attended Loos' 'lecture with slides', the Council were still demanding 'a decorated facade', but the session forced them to reduce this to an undertaking that window-boxes be added and a guarantee be given of 'lively flowers all year round'.

The show's only complete original environment was appropriately from Loos. As the Map Guide indicates, he was the most omnipresent influence on the domestic environment of the Viennese professional classes at this time – prolific because his manner suited their tastes, and as many anecdotal accounts record, his work outlasted changing fashion in its deep humanism as well as its sheer quality of craftsmanship. The 'sitting corner', **above,** comprised original furniture from Loos' apartment of 1901-2 for the Turnowskys, in today's Gusshausstrasse. Such comfortable conversation niches of fixed and loose seating were standard elements of the Loos domestic interior. The rich sensitivity to highest-quality natural materials was equally manifested in his own sartorial taste. In Kokoschka's portrait of 1909, **centre below,** the three-piece suit is ruffled with latent action, but the typically smooth English tweed overcoat appears in the 1918 photograph **below left,** with Peter Altenberg, in whose company he was a well-known frequenter of Vienna's nightlife.

The extraordinary expansion of the tiny space of the American Bar, right and opposite, of 1908 (3.5x7m), probably owed as much to his intimate familiarity with the type as to general architectural skill. **Right:** the interior slightly modified with seating. **Opposite:** the new exterior of original materials made for the exhibition, and for eventual reinstatement of the bar's exterior, on research by Herman Czech. With chronological exactitude, it formed the doorway from the Turnowsky interior to the Michaelerplatz room and Chicago tower.

The Klimt room, entered through a gilded doorway, right, from the dark natural materials of Loos' haut-bourgeois interior. An annexe through the white doorway, left, contained a range of Secessionist painting both from those who would break away with Klimt in 1905 to present their work with the designers in the Kunstschauen of 1908 and 9, and from the more conservative rump who remained 'pure painters'

'Pallas Athene'
1898

'Nuda Veritas'
1899
Initially purchased
by Secessionist theorist and
propagandist, Hermann Bahr

'Hoffnung II'
1907-8

Portrait of
Sonia Knips
1898

under Josef Engelhart. That room was hung in a conventional manner, not by Hollein, and thereby heightened the qualities of the main sequence. In the 1908 Kunstschau as here, Gustav Klimt had the largest room devoted to a single artist. On this main wall, the chronology moves inwards from both sides to the centre, focusing on paintings which were most seminal for the development of his language and technique.

Portrait of
Adele Bloch-Bauer, I,
1907

'Judith and
Holofernes'
1901

Portrait of
Emilie Flöge, his mistress
and sister-in-law
1902

'Waternymphs'
1899

GUSTAV KLIMT
■ & THE SECESSIONIST PAINTERS ■

The spread on the preceding pages conveys the simplicity and spaciousness of Hollein's design for the Klimt room, contrasted by Hollein himself to 'the curator's approach' to hanging. As elsewhere, it is an interpretation of a period environment, indeed probably a synthesis of two. The extreme simplicity is most redolent of the XVIII Secession show of 1903, devoted entirely to Klimt. This was designed by Kolo Moser, who as Christian Nebehay has rightly noted in this connection, 'has up to now been far too little appreciated as the pioneer of exhibition technique that he was.' Held in the Secession building, the most elaborate element of his design was the chairs, which appear on page 44 above. The second source is certainly the Klimt room – number 22, and the largest – at the first Kunstschau of 1908, when Hoffmann's grand temporary buildings for the breakaway 'Klimt group' (see page 42 above), housed painting, architecture and Wiener Werkstätte design in an integrated presentation. Here was not only the same strong skirting-board delineation of the floor as previously, but a decorative wall treatment of scattered squares on a square grid, which is reflected in Hollein's gold frieze, and also a strong geometrical pattern over the doorways creating a floor-to-ceiling 'panel', which is reflected as an abstract spatial element in Hollein's diagonal corner panels.

Subtlety of the grouping of works around each of the three exits to the room is shown in these three views. **Above,** the threshold to the generally more naturalistic and figurative work in the Secessionist annexe is flanked, *left,* by a selection of Klimt's most conventionally pictorial, that is less flattened and abstracted works, from the Wartime years 1916-18. *From the extreme left they are:* 'The Baby', 1917-18, and two 'Portraits of a woman' from 1916-17 and 1917-18. Through the doorway appears part of a Schiele townscape. On the Klimts to the right of the doorway, see preceding page.

The sequence of the main wall continues **opposite top,** *left.* Juxtaposed to the ultra-urban image of Loos' Chicago Tribune column are two of Klimt's most idyllically rural landscapes, 'Roses under trees', c.1905, and 'Park' of 1910.

With the build-up of his mature style behind the viewer, on the main wall, the greatest easel painting of that style blazes through the next doorway at maximum power by being framed with earlier works. A very interesting sequence in their own right, being generally little known, these formed a diversion on which it was hard to delay once the eye had been caught by 'The Kiss'. First shown in that room at the 1908 Kunstschau, this painting received the extraordinary accolade of being bought for the nation even before the show closed. The early paintings are, *left to right:* on the landscape wall: 'Still Pond', 1899; on the corner panel: 'Hermione Gallia', 1903-4; left of the doorway: 'Love', 1895, which was the starting point for themes of 'The Kiss' in his oeuvre; 'Fabel', a historicist work as reminder of the Makart influence, from 1883, and an early venture into abstraction called 'Rough Water', 1898.

Right of the doorway are the intimately scaled 'Portrait of a woman', thought to be Frau Heyman, of 1894; the watercolour 'Interior of the Old Burgtheater' of 1888-9 and another little historical allegory of the same years called 'Sappho'. Paired opposite the respectable naturalism of Ms. Gallia, on the corner panel, is the cheeky and buxom nude with her 'Golden Fish', painted a year previously. And the patterned green forms, simultaneously water and weed, re-emerge almost a decade later in the quieter paintwork of 'Kammer Castle at Altersee, III', 1910, extreme right: visually immaculate hanging and a rare economy of selection.

53

Opposite, *right of picture:* the reconstruction of Hoffmann's design for the side gallery of the Secession building at the XIV Exhibition, 15 April to 27 June 1902, devoted to celebrating the Leipzig artist Max Klinger's recently completed statue of Beethoven. As the catalogue's Foreword said, 'May this exhibition thus be an act of hommage to Max Klinger, who both through his creative activity and through his writings has illuminated our whole view of art.' *Right foreground:* Klinger's vast original sculpture is represented by his half-sized marble copy of the upper portion of the figure itself, made in c.1906 for the music room of Carl Wittgenstein's home and bought by its present owners, the Boston Museum of Fine Arts, from the pianist Paul Wittgenstein.
Above: inside the reconstructed room containing Klimt's frieze on themes of Beethoven's Ninth Symphony. Over the entrance, *right,* are the themes, *left to right,* of 'Art', 'The Choir of Heavenly Angels Singing of the Joy of God', and 'The Kiss of the Whole World' – the latter being another stage in the development towards Klimt's ultimate 'Kiss', which is visible below it. Through Hoffmann's screen wall, *centre,* is a look forward in time to Franz Ferdinand's catafalque and the grim anti-lyricism of Egger-Leinz's 'Nameless Ones' of the First World War's battlefields.

THE BEETHOVEN FRIEZE

Klimt's 'Kiss', painted during 1901-2, stood as a free-standing altarpiece to sensuality between two contrasting moods: *to the right,* the sunny uplands of the Secessionist dream in one of its most deeply felt moments of Gesamtkunstwerk, with hints of its less spiritual passions in a corner behind; *to the left,* already the threat of a darkness that would extinguish it.

Few pictures are better calculated to draw the viewer across a space, especially when backed up by the next generation's scandal of Schiele's 'Seated Male Nude' of 1910. Around the 'altarpiece' was a summary of the transfer from older generation to new which was catalysed by the Kunstschauen. Young Kokoschka was brought into the first, in 1908, and Schiele to the second in 1909. Here Schiele's 'Seated Male Nude', one of his first major ventures into such explicitness, was the invitation into a discrete and suitably intimate annexe on the right, (at the same time, it could be said, suggestively long and thin), which showed a selection of his sometimes cool, sometimes highly erotic little figures in pen and watercolour.

From the diagonal corner screen the older generation was looking down the slot, in the person of Kokoschka's 1913 portrait of Carl Moll, and from the perpendicular wall, left, the funnelling movement was completed by Schiele's own 'Embrace' of 1917 – a promise and summary of the pleasures to be found there. Again it was masterly selection and hanging for recounting the artistic episode.

Thus drawn to the far end of the central ground-floor gallery, the visitor was in a position to understand that he stood in the central hall of the Secession building; that it was early summer 1902, and that we were celebrating Beethoven. A plan and photographs of that original installation accompany Hollein's description of the related events, and of this reconstruction of Klimt's 'Beethoven room', in his article above.

Klimt's Beethoven room looking towards the exit, with Hoffmann's own abstract sopraporta relief reconstructed over the steps. As Hollein describes in his article on the reconstructions and as his documentary photograph shows, a small Klinger sculpture of a girl's head stood in front of the pillar by the exit steps, and decorative panels which were not now traceable occupied the square niches to the left. In Klimt's frieze, *left wall*, naked figures of 'Frail, suffering Humanity' make supplications to 'Well-armoured Strength' in the presence of 'Compassion and Ambition'. *On the end wall:* 'The Hostile Powers' stand waiting, with right, the lonely figure of 'Gnawing Grief'. *Right wall:* flying figures 'Yearning for Happiness' find 'Gratification in Poetry'. *Lower right:* the front view of Klinger's 'Beethoven'.

'The Hostile Powers', *left to right*, of Disease, Madness, Death, Lust, Unchastity and Intemperance.

The elaborately dressed hair of 'Intemperance' is a particularly rich example of Klimt's use of applique materials to give relief and sparkle at certain focal points of the painted composition, and representing a transitional stage towards the full mosaic of the Stoclet frieze. Here the materials used are buttons of pressed metal and mother-of-pearl, curtain rings, tacks and bits of mirror. When executed, the work was of course expected to be temporary.

'Gnawing Grief' and the butt ends of Hoffmann's gilded beams

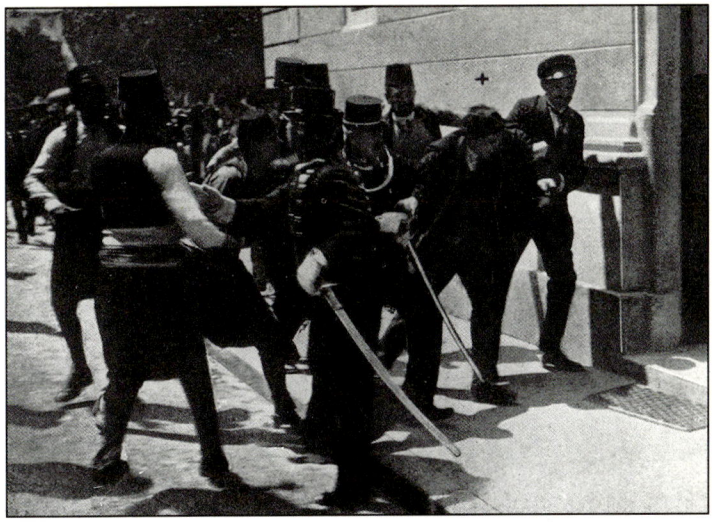

ASSASSINATION & SOCIALISM

Top: Documentary photographs of street-scenes in Bosnia just before and after the assassination of Archduke Franz-Ferdinand, 28 June 1914, which precipitated the start of the First World War. **Opposite**: Winterhalter's confident Empress Elizabeth of 1864, the ghost of a simpler past beside the catafalque with Franz-Ferdinand's blood-stained uniform, and Albin Egger-Lienz's 'Nameless Ones 1914', of 1916. Around them, framed Declarations of War in perfect diplomatic French. A video enacts scenes from Karl Kraus's *Last Days of Mankind*. In a gilded 'box' a page of Ludwig Wittgenstein's manuscript for the *Tractatus logico-philosophicus*, written during Wartime military service, its strange lighting evoking the other, anti-rational, pole of intellectual life in Freud upstairs. Inside the inscription from Wittgenstein '*Wovon man nicht sprechen kann, darüber muss man schweigen*' (What a man cannot express in language he must keep silent about). **Above**: the Post-War socialist housing programme: a proletarian apartment drawn full-size in pink carpet.

Red Vienna of the 1920s:
Achievements of the Socialists' 1923 Housing Act, which the graphics of 1930 depict as the Proletarian equivalent of the Imperial Ringstrasse project. Photographs and drawings, *left and centre*, show the Karl-Marx-Hof (Map Guide no. 76), location of the worker's apartment drawn in the carpet. Other developments featured include Map Guide nos. 11, 28, 121, 129, 132. *Foreground*: Realist sculpture by Anton Hanak, *left*, 'The Burning Man' and *right*, 'The Last Man', of 1922. 'Torso', *left*, of 1929, by his pupil Fritz Wotruba.

Towards a darker reality

Clockwise from left:

● Poster by Friedrich Kiesler for the International Exhibition of New Theatre Techniques at the Konzerthaus, Vienna, 1924.
● At the International Art Exhibition organised by the Secession in 1924: works by emigré Russians including Chagall, Naum Gabo, *centre*, and Kandinsky, *right*.
● Willi Forst and Marlene Dietrich in a typically torrid scene from *Café Elektric*, 1927.
● A poster summoning 'Men and women of Vienna' to a 'giant protest rally' against Ernst Krenek's opera *Jonny spielt auf* which had its premier on 31 December 1927. 'Our State Operahouse' says the poster, 'the leading artistic and cultural centre of the world, the pride of Vienna, has fallen victim to desecration by this bit of Jewish-Negro insolence, *Jonny spielt auf*.' Organisers of the protest were the National Socialist German Worker's Party.
● Poster for the first production of Alban Berg's opera *Wozzeck* in Vienna in March 1930. It was a sign of Vienna's movement away from the artistic front-line that this full-length atonal opera, whose Berlin debut was already five years past, became the object of public ridicule and constant scandal in Vienna that year.
● 'Free wood from the Augarten' – the unemployed, many of them middle-class and professional people, reduced to cutting firewood in Vienna's public parks during the Depression. Documentary photograph, 1930, by S Wagner.

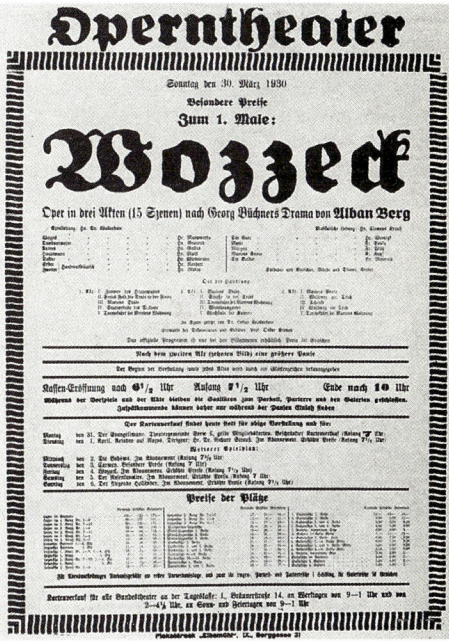

Red and black arts:
As the first schemes were going up under the new socialist housing programme, left-liberals were bringing the arts of revolutionary Russia to the centre of public attention. 1924 saw two major shows. The International Exhibition of New Theatre Techniques lauded the latest work of the Stenbergs, Exter, Alexander Vesnin in their collaborations with Mayerkhold and Tairov. Instigator of that show was the stage designer Friedrich Kiesler, and it proved a debut for his 'Informal-Support-System' of Constructivist-inspired display structures. One of these was reconstructed for *Dream and Reality*, **left,** by Thomas Weingraber.

Whilst Kiesler had the previous year joined Hans Richter and El Lissitsky to launch their Constructivist magazine *G*, his fellow producer Max Reinhardt marked 1924 with productions at his Theatre in der Josefstadt designed by Oskar Laske (see Map guide no 108) and founder Secessionist Alfred Roller, neither of whose styles had changed greatly since pre-War. When the Werkbund architect Oskar Strnad designed *Das Mirakel* for Reinhardt in 1927 it was no less realistic. Still extant as an exhibiting society, the Secession had organised the 1924 International Art Show that also featured Russians. The slogan of Kiesler's colleague in the Hungarian *MA* group Bela Uitz, however, that 'Politics and art belong together' was to be a sentiment that backfired on the progressives as the Depression and Nazism blacked out the sky. Only the world of Dietrich, in Hollein's words 'stretching her leg to adjust her stocking', could offer much levity or an echo of the old sensuality.

STUART DURANT
THE AUSTRIAN WERKBUND

Monogram of the German Werkbund, from their Yearbook, 1915

Monogram of the Austrian Werkbund, designed by Rudolf von Larisch

THE ÖSTERREICHISCHER WERKBUND FOUNDED IN 1912, seems to symbolise Mitteleuropa's desire to follow in Germany's footsteps. The successes, triumphs even, of the Deutscher Werkbund had not passed unnoticed in Viennese commercial and artistic circles.

Germany's first economic miracle occurred in the early years of this century. By the second decade of the twentieth century Germany had already secured a share of world trade which was surpassed only by that of the United States. Read Pogge von Strandmann's recently published translation of Walther Rathenau's diaries if you want to savour the heady atmosphere of the period: Rathenau of AEG was the patron of Peter Behrens.

The founding of the Deutscher Werkbund, in October 1907, was a demonstration of Germany's awareness of her own extraordinary industrial potential, as well as her simultaneous acknowledgement of her vulnerability to foreign competition. The purpose of the Werkbund, it will be remembered, was to improve the quality of German manufactured goods 'through the combined efforts of artists, industrialists and craftsmen'. The idea of quality, in its widest sense, began to preoccupy industrialists and designers. Good design came to be seen as an essential attribute of *qualität* – quality. Germany's captive market was too small for her ambitions. Her colonial empire was not impressive when compared with Britain's. If Germany was to continue her economic and cultural advance, her manufactures had to be produced to the highest possible standards. A forum in which to debate issues of design and production was called for. The Deutscher Werkbund successfully provided such a forum.

Austrians were to play an important part in the German Werkbund from its earliest days. Among the 971 individual and corporate members listed in the first Werkbund Yearbook of 1912 are to be found some 76 Austrians – as well as numbers of Hungarians and Czechs. Among Austrian architects who had joined the German Werkbund were to be found: Josef Frank, Josef Hoffmann, Heinrich Kathrein, Ernst Lichtblau, Robert Oerley, Dagobert Peche, Cesar Poppovits, Otto Prutscher, Oskar Strnad and Otto Wagner. In 1912, Wagner was already aged seventy-one, while Hoffmann, at forty-one, was at the very peak of his powers. Of the rest, the majority were in their twenties or thirties. Painters and decorative designers who had joined included: Ferdinand Andri, Franz Çizek, Gustav Klimt, Berthold Löffler, Koloman Moser, Michael Powolny and Alfred Roller. Roller had been elected to the Werkbund committee, and the Wiener Werkstätte had taken out corporate membership.

The Österreichischer Werkbund was inaugurated on June 7th, 1912. Adolf Feiherr von Bachofen, an industrialist, was elected president; its vice-president was Alexander Pazzani, who was the managing director of the Poldihütte steel company. Among the leading members of the Austrian Werkbund committee were: Hoffmann, Franz Klein the former Minister of Justice and Stephen Rath of the Lobmeyr glass manufactory. Cizek, Oerley, Powolny, Prutscher, Strnad and Carl Witzmann, an architect and a professor at the Kunstgewerbeschule were also committee members. (How quickly an avant garde had metamorphosed into an establishment). Josef Zasche, a Prague architect, was the Czech representative. The setting up of the Austrian branch of the Werkbund is documented in the German Werkbund Yearbook of 1914.

By 1916 the Austrian Werkbund had 637 members, including companies which had taken out corporate membership. Almost all the leading Austrian architects and designers joined, as well as several leading painters. Czechs and Hungarians were well represented. Adolf Loos would have nothing to do with the Werkbund, as one might have expected. Nor had Kokoschka joined. Surprisingly, the playwright Hugo von Hofmannsthal had.

Almost twenty per cent of the membership was female – 124 women members in all. Interestingly this was a much higher proportion than in the German Werkbund. Some of the women members were evidently the wives of male members, but the majority were art workers in their own right. Among these were: Mathilde Flögl, a graphic artist and muralist, Lotte Frömmel-Fochler, a textile designer, Rosa Neuwirth, a decorative ceramicist who had been born in Prague, Marie Schmid, a calligrapher and assistant lecturer at the Kunstgewerbeschule

Left, embroidered dresses by Emmy Zweybrück-Prochaska, Austrian pavilion, Werkbund Exhibition, Cologne, 1914, *GW Yearbook* 1915. **Above**, Rudolf Grimm, Vienna tramway shelters, *GW Yearbook* 1914. **Below**, Robert Oerley, House in Kalksburg, garden front; **below left**, anon, student study of barn structure (both Eisler).

and the embroiderer Emmy Zweybrück-Prochaska.

In the first German Werkbund Yearbook of 1912, which had retrospectively surveyed work of members, Austria had been particularly well represented. Hoffmann's handsome classicising villa of 1912 for Eduard Ast, a specialist in concrete construction, is prominently featured. Also illustrated in the 1912 Yearbook are ceramic figures by Powolny and interiors by Carl Witzmann. There were, in addition, illustrations of fashion designs by Edward Wimmer (later Wimmer-Wisgrill), who was a pupil of Koloman Moser, a versatile designer in the applied arts, as well as an architect. Here Vienna was following a trend that seems to have started with Henry Van de Velde, the first modern architect, apparently, to have dabbled in fashion design: photographs of dresses he designed appear in the May 1902 number of Alexander Koch's *Kunst und Dekoration*. It was no doubt felt by the editors of the 1912 yearbook, that illustrations of Austrian work would enhance the Werkbund's status internationally.

For whatever reasons, Austria was barely represented in the 1913 Werkbund Yearbook – merely illustrations of the Wiener Werkstätte showrooms in Karlsbad, by Hoffmann. The 1914 Yearbook was devoted principally to bridges, locomotives, aircraft, battleships and ocean liners – areas of manufacture and design in which, one must concede, Austria was not strong. Nevertheless, sophisticated prefabricated passenger shelters for the Vienna tramway system, designed by Rudolf Grimm, were shown. Also illustrated was a railway station

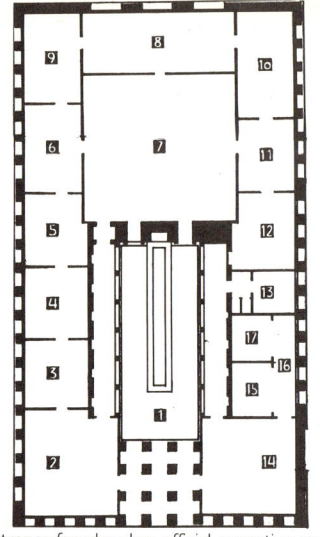

Austrian Pavilion, Werkbund Exhibition, Cologne, 1914: Hoffmann's building: entrance facade; plan; official reception room (with J. Soulek) (Eisler).

Arts and Crafts room, designed by Carl Witzman (*GW Yearbook* 1915)

Otto Prutscher and Thonet Bros: reception room furniture (Eisler)

Otakar Novotny, Czech Werkbund room showing Czech Cubist influence (Eisler)

booking hall by Heinrich Kathrein, owing something to Otto Wagner's Post Office Savings Bank of 1904-06. Kolomon Moser's florid banknotes in the graphic style of *Ver Sacrum*, the Secessionist journal founded in 1898, are disappointing.

The great showcase for Werkbund achievements was the Werkbund Austellung which was held in Cologne in 1914. This exhibition is very fully illustated in the next yearbook *Deutsche Form im Kriegsjahr. Jahrbuch des Deutschen Werkbundes*, of 1915. The impact of what has subsequently been recognised as one of the most important events in the history of the Modern Movement was virtually nullified at the time by the outbreak of war in August. However, historians have been fixated by what went on in Cologne in 1914, ever since Pevsner published *Pioneers of the Modern Movement* in 1936, twenty-two years after the event. The main reason for this, of course, was the existence of Gropius' model factory in which some of the characteristic features of Modern Movement architecture made their appearance, it is said, for the first time. Gropius' model factory created – how can one put it? – a retrospective sensation. Pevsner actually said of it: 'Never since the Sainte Chapelle and the choir of Beaulieu had the human art of building been so triumphant over matter'. Such hyperbole now has a quaint old-fashioned flavour. Theodor Fischer's assertive block-like pavilion for Heinersdorf – makers of stained glass and mosaic – and Bruno Taut's expressionistic, proto-geodesic Glashaus have also caused retroactive excitement. Both buildings would have been entirely at home in Paris in 1925 – in the Art Déco exhibition.

Among the members of the organizing committee of the Cologne 1914 exhibition were: Behrens, Fischer, Gropius, Muthesius, Bruno Paul, Riemerschmid and Van der Velde. It is difficult to conceive of a more glittering assembly of proto-moderns. The Austrian Werkbund was represented on the committee by Hoffmann and Alfred Roller

Hoffmann & Soulek, room of the Poldihütte Steel Company (Eisler)

Hamburg section, by Vienna-trained Carl Otto Czeschka (*GW Yearbook*, 1915)

Hoffmann with Kohn Bros: sixteen types of bentwood chair (*GW Yearbook*, 1915)

Wiener Werkstätte room: Wimmer fashions, Leopold Loevy furnishings (Eisler)

who had been one of the founders of the Vienna Secession and who, in 1914, was director of the Kunstgewerbeschule and the leading theatrical designer in Vienna.

Hoffmann was the designer of the Austrian pavilion, the Österreichisches Haus at the Cologne exhibition. It was given pride of place in the 1915 Werkbund Yearbook. This temporary building, which fits awkwardly into the history of the Modern Movement, has never quite received the attention it deserves from historians. Hoffmann paraphrases the Graeco-Roman temple. The Austrian pavilion consisted, in fact, of two adjacent temple-like structures which were linked by a porch and peristyle. Otto Wagner, Hoffmann's mentor, was also an exponent of modernised classicism. Leafing through the pages of the Wagnerschule Yearbooks we observe how he encouraged his students to design in this manner. Behrens, in several of his buildings for AEG, also applied the classical formula. Both Muthesius and Bruno Taut designed pavilions in a more or less classical idiom for Cologne. But a certain theatricality, or perhaps I should say 'sense of occasion', separates Hoffmann's pavilion from the other classicising buildings in the 1914 exhibition. Hoffmann's Österreichisches Haus has authority which characterises his best work.

Visitors in the Österreichisches Haus saw what was probably the best collection of Viennese applied art ever brought together. Neither *Dream and Reality* nor any other recent exhibition could compete with the Österreichisches Haus. Here, for the visitors to Cologne to study, was the current taste of the cultivated Viennese middle class – a class which could enjoy sensuous opulence, but which was able to avoid the vulgarity which had been seen in Paris in the 1900 Universal Exhibition: a middle class which could appear to be refined, without being prim. In all this one is reminded, a little, of Britain in the 1870s and 1880s – the era of the Aesthetic Movement – when the bourgeois millenium seemed to

Houses by Josef Frank and his associates: above left, a suburban house, from Eisler 1916. Frank's student thesis had been a study of Alberti and a classical spirit — if not sometimes explicit references — was always mixed with the free-style elements (*cf* Map Guide nos 18, 38 also Strnad & Wlach, no 41). **Above**, an interior showing strong influences of English Arts and Crafts work in both spirit and individual items of furniture. This is attributed to Frank by Eisler, but appears to be the living room of the Cobenzlgasse house (1910-12, Map Guide 41), now more firmly attributed to his partners Strnad and Wlach. **Left**, suburban house, one of the pair designed with Strnad and Wlach on Wilbrandtgasse (1913-14, Map Guide no 38; see p 76 where its street facade is also ilustrated).

have arrived. But the design of the Aesthetic period was often affected and thus all too vulnerable to the barbs of satirists. The work of Austrian Werkbund members, on the other hand, was taken very seriously in 1914. Only later did Modernist historians begin to claim that Viennese design was a trifle frivolous and that Hoffmann, for all his gifts, did not deserve to be mentioned in the same breath as Gropius.

There was great consistency in the Austrian Werkbund applied art on display in Cologne. Such homogeneity does not, however, imply unadventurous conformity. Rather, it indicates Vienna's confidence in having arrived at an appropriate twentieth century style. Had not the war, which shattered the brittle alliances of Mitteleuropa, interrupted developments, it is entirely reasonable to suggest that the history of twentieth century architecture, certainly design in the applied arts, would have taken a different course from the one we know all too well. For Austrian Proto-Modernism was less dogmatic, less inflexible, than its German equivalent.

The achievements of the Austrian Werkbund are probably best studied in the volume *Österreichische Werkkultur* which was published in 1916. This official publication of the Österreicher Werkbund was edited by a critic and university lecturer, Max Eisler. The book has exactly the same format as the Werkbund Yearbooks. But it is much closer in feeling to the Yearbooks published by the *Studio* journal in London during the years just before the First World War — the period when the dominant aesthetic ideology in Britain was that of the Arts and Crafts Movement. *Österreichische Werkkultur*, which contains almost five hundred illustrations, is an incomparable record of Viennese design in its mature phase. I reproduce several of its illustrations here.

The theme of this Austrian Werkbund book was the home and accoutrements — the villa of the Viennese burgess to be exact. The theme was a poignant one, for chaos was the leitmotiv of the day. But one senses little of the war in the book. One observes merely an illustration of a tumbler decorated with the flags of Austria, Germany and Turkey, designed by Hoffmann, and showrooms for the Poldihütte Company, also by Hoffmann, with artillery shells displayed like minimalist sculptures. Houses by Oskar Strnad and Josef Frank (of Strnad, Wlach and Frank, Wollzeile 45, Vienna I) are of particular interest. A villa by Strnad — a professor in the Kunstgewerbeschule — possess some of the characteristics of a house by Voysey, with overtones of Palladio. Frank is the more interesting of the two architects — a town villa of his has the gauntness of an early Loos building and is coolly matter-of-fact.

But the war, the hideous war from which Europe has yet to recover, put paid to a series of remarkable experiments in architecture and the applied arts. The Viennese style was enjoyable — if not populist — in the way that the International Style never was. Its comparatively recent rediscovery — which began in the mid nineteen-sixties — is part of our continuing search for an architectural mode which is learned as well as pleasurable. Vienna still has much to teach us.

Werkbund furniture for different social classes and environments, from Eisler, 1916: **Above**, Lorenz Bogataj, manufacturer, furniture for a working class home. The idea of producing well-designed furniture for working families was comparatively radical in 1916: Heal's 'cottage furniture' of similar date in England, for example, was intended for a middle-class clientele. **Above left**, Ferdinand Steiner and Adolf Jiretz, furniture for a minor civil servant's home. It is interesting to see how the precise social distinctions of Austro-Hungarian society manifested themselves in a Werkbund publication. **Left**, Josef Hoffmann, W. Hollmann, cabinetmaker, entrance lounge to the offices of Poldihütte Steel Company. Artillery shells on the window sill and rear display are a reminder of the appalling war in which Austria was engaged in 1916. **Below left**, Fritz and A. Nagel, an office and its furnishings, in a simplicity that looks forward to Art Deco and beyond.

References: The principal documentary sources referred to in this article, whence the illustrations also derive, are as follows: **1** *Yearbooks of the German Werkbund*, from 1912-15 (referred to in captions as GW Yearbooks). The richest source on Austrian material is that for 1915 *(Deutsche Form im Kriegsjahr. Jahrbuch des Deutschen Werkbundes*, 1915). **2** The survey collection edited by Max Eisler, entitled *Österreichische Werkkultur. Herausgegeben vom Österreichischen Werkbund*, published by Anton Schroll, Vienna 1916 (referred to in captions as Eisler). Following its recent restoration, the Austrian Werkbund's later model Siedlung project (Map Guide no 7), has also now been fully documented in : Adolf Krischanitz and Otto Kapfinger, *Die Wiener Werkbundsiedlung: Dokumentation einer Erneuerung*, Compress Verlag, Vienna, 1985.

CATHERINE COOKE MAP GUIDE VIENNA 1870-1930

ALMOST TWENTY YEARS AGO HANS HOLLEIN CONTRIBUTED the Vienna material to that classic first series of *AD* Map Guides on which a generation of us travelled Europe in the 1960s. In 103 buildings his list covered the period from 1600 to its publication date of October 1969. It remains of particular interest for its detail on work then current, and readers are also referred to it for all architecture before 1870.

The present guide focuses in detail on the period defined by the *Dream and Reality* exhibition, that is roughly 1870-1930. In architectural terms it starts with the Ringstrasse and ends with the Austrian Werkbund's model housing estate of 1930-32. In the latter year, the rising supremacy of the post-Secessionist generation was forcefully marked by Hoffmann's abandonment of the original Werkbund to Josef Frank and the debates on Neue Sachlichkeit. It was also the year when the Wiener Werkstätte finally closed. As Frank later wrote to Eduard Sekler, it was 'entirely inappropriate for these impoverished conditions'.

For ease of location, numbering of buildings here follows the usual format of reading left-to-right across the map. Two particularly dense areas, Hietzing and the Inner City are enlarged; on the latter plan Ringstrasse buildings are marked by stars. Local streets are shown only in the environs of marked buildings, and for navigation this sketch-map should be complemented by a city-plan such as Falk's. Essential transport information by *U-bahn* is included here.

On the one architect for whom a full *catalogue raisonné* does exist, namely Hoffmann, all buildings are referred to that catalogue thus: 'ES cat.', the source being: E. Sekler, *Josef Hoffmann. The Architectural Work* (Princeton, 1985). On certain Loos works I refer to the book of his assistant Heinrich Kulka, *viz*: H. Kulka, *Adolf Loos. Das Werk des Architekten* (Vienna, 1930 & 1979), and in respect of Plečnik to: Damian Prelövšek, *Josef Plečnik, Wiener Arbeiten von 1896 bis 1914* (Vienna, 1979).

For help during preparation of this guide I am particularly grateful to Paul Melbinger, for discussion and much footslog around Viennese streets, and to Doris Orr-Meyer in Cambridge. My thanks also go to Otto Kapfinger and Herman Czech for checking the result.

Outside the Ringstrasse – West

1 Purkersdorf Sanatorium 1903-5. JOSEF HOFFMANN
Purkersdorf, Wiener Strasse 74
U: to Hütteldorf and Bahn to Unter-Purkersdorf
A luxurious sanatorium for nervous disorders and therapy under the smart Dr Viktor Zuckerkandl, with every latest treatment and general comfort, called Westend. Set in large park. Construction of reinforced concrete, fully exploited for its geometric simplicity both outside and in. The abstract, layered relief of original main facade entirely spoiled by Leopold Bauer in adding extra storey in 1926 with pitched roof, destroying dramatic central window of stairhall and the ceramic blue and white chequered banding of window apertures, used here for first time by Hoffmann. Originally entirely fitted out by the Wiener Werkstätte as their first project on that scale; chairs etc by Moser and Hoffmann. Virtually all interior details gone; building stands empty and sad. (ES cat 84).

2 Second Villa Wagner 1913-14 OTTO WAGNER
XIV, Hüttelbergstrasse 28 *U: Hütteldorf*
A second suburban villa for his last years very close to that of his youth, and equally typical of its period. Above the half-basement are *bel étage* and second floor with a long flight of stairs leading straight up to the former from the front door, and a 'private' stair in the diagonally opposite corner leading above and below. Dining room occupies the whole main frontage, with only service hall, entrance lounge and open loggia on this floor. Near-cubic volume and ironwork is equally simple. All richness is in the blue and white geometrical tilework with aluminium fixing bolts at main floor level and around the flat, porchless, front door. Polychrome glass mosaics in and above the door executed by Wiener Werkstätte workshops under Leopold Forstner. Stained glass window above the door, lighting the stair, and also mosaic frieze in loggia, by Kolo Moser.

3 First Villa Wagner 1886-8 OTTO WAGNER
XIV, Hüttelbergstrasse 26 *U: Hütteldorf*
Idyllically set in the grand manner on a wooded hillside just off the road, and approached by sweeping driveways and symmetrical double staircases. Giant order of the central loggia combines with strong overhanging eaves and pergolas L & R, to give extraordinary scale to a small if luxurious house. Pergola L enclosed to form studio in 1900, with stained glass windows by Adolf Böhm; pergola R enclosed as sitting room in 1895. Now the home of painter Ernst Fuchs, who has developed decoration in his own spirit whilst restoring the whole house and opening it to the public (see *Art & Design* February 1986 pp 6-9).

4 Villa Vojcsik 1901 OTTO SCHÖNTAL
XIV, Linzer Strasse 375 *U: Hütteldorf*
This Wagner pupil builds on his own before joining the master's office in 1902 (*cf* also no.133). Splendid Jugendstil street architecture in a four windowed, three storey central 'pavilion' with lower elements L & R. Colour from broad polychrome banding of stylised fruits. Has lost a certain bounce where straight horizontals have replaced curves in surface treatment of attic and basement (perhaps in the late 1970s renovation and interior redesign by Boris Podrecca?), but still highly enjoyable.

5 Stoessl House 1911-12 ADOLF LOOS
XIII, Matrasgasse 20 *U: Ober St Veit*
A modest and economical house for Dr Otto and Mrs Auguste Stoessl totalling four floors on a sloping garden site. Conventionally villa-like looks belie unusual and ingenious planning. The two storey mansard gives maximum living space for fabric cost, the upper floor being the library, with half-round dormers, the lower one the main living room, which gives onto a full-width inset rear verandah overlooking the garden.

6 Hermann Bahr's House 1899-1900
JOSEPH MARIA OLBRICH
XIII, Winzerstrasse 22 *U: Ober St Veit*
For the Secession's main theorist and critical champion. Rectangular house with very high-pitched tiled roof through which peep tiny dormer lights. Slightly altered, but embodying his concept of 'the small house' that in Hevesi's words 'has sprung up out of the living soil', 'protective' as Bahr himself said 'in a way, that only the threatened German peasant can understand'. Intended to be a prototype for a series of houses in the Hohe Warte district that were realised after Olbrich's departure to Darmstadt (late 1899) by Hoffmann (Spitzer, Moser & Moll houses, nos 74, 75).

7 Werkbund Siedlung 1930-32 coordinator JOSEF FRANK
XIII, Veitingergasse, Jagdschlossgasse Woinovichgasse
U: Hietzing then streetcar 60
Settlement of mainly two storey housing, some villas, some terraces, conceived on the Weissenhof model. Planned in 1930 as parallel event to the Austrian Werkbund Exhibition laid on for the 19th Congress of the German Werkbund held in Vienna that year, though not completed until summer 1932. By that time the Austrian group had undergone a major split between Hoffmann and the Sachlichkeit adherents lead by Frank, who was coordinator here. Some losses in World War II (Sobotka, Strnad), but remainder mostly restored. On a compact triangular site, the most interesting extant work is as follows: Veitingergasse 71 & 73 by HUGO HÄRING; 79-85 by JOSEF HOFFMANN (ES cat. 333); 87-93 by ANDRÉ LURÇAT; 99 & 101 by OSKAR WLACH; 107-9 by ERNST PLISCHKE; 115 & 117 by OSWALD HAERDTL. Behind these; the first pair on Jagdschlossgasse, by ERNST LICHTBLAU. In Woinovichgasse, 2 & 4 by MARGARETE LIHOTZKY; 9 by RICHARD NEUTRA; 13-19 by ADOLF LOOS & HEINRICH KULKA; 14-20 by GERRIT RIETVELD; end of terrace facing these, pair by CLEMENS HOLZMEISTER; 32 by JOSEF FRANK. Recent renovaton with original polychrome etc and small museum by Krischanitz & Kapfinger.

Purkersdorf, original entrance with ceramic relief panels by Richard Luksch, from The Studio special issue, 1906.

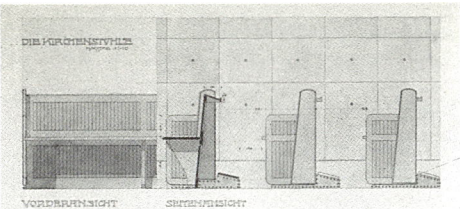

Wagner's drawing for the Steinhof church pews (photo Pirker, courtesy Hollein).

8 Church am Steinhof 1905-7 OTTO WAGNER
XIV, Baumgartner Höhe 1 on Sanatoriumstrasse
U: Volkstheater then bus 48A
Church of St Leopold within the Lower Austrian Mental Hospital, laid out on the lines of Wagner's 1902 competition plan, though only the church eventually built by him (see colour photos pp 18-19, 21). The general form of a smooth half-circular dome rising between four cubic corner towers was a development of earlier unbuilt church designs, for Berlin Cathedral in 1891 and the Capuchine Church conversion in 1898.
Most exterior metalwork is copper or coppered iron, and now green like the dome which was originally gilded. For certain functional details of the interior, (heating, pews, sloped floor) see p 21. The extensive stained glass side windows lighting the main space are Kolo Moser. Mosaic work behind the altar by Remigius Geyling in mixed materials, finished 1913. Altar furniture and baldacchino by Wagner, though kneeling angels in bas-relief and other decorative elements by Othmar Schimkowitz, who also did the angels on the four columns of the main porch outside. Local saints on the four corner towers outside by Richard Luksch. A long walk up from the road, tours 3pm Sat.

9 Heuberg Siedlung 1921 ADOLF LOOS
XVII, Kretschekgasse, Röntgengasse, Schrammelgasse, Plachygasse & Trenkwaldgasse
U: Schottentor then streetcar 2 (also bus 44B)
Settlement planned and built whilst Loos was Chief Architect to the Vienna Housing Department (1920-22) on his principles (supervised by Hugo Mayer). Workers' two storey terraced houses on square plans run back into deep allotments and integral greenhouses, for self-sufficiency in face of post-war inflation. Loos' patented 'house of one wall', ie terraces of timber spans and cladding between concrete cross-walls, applied most rigorously in the terrace running form Röntgengasse 138 to Plachygasse 1-13.

10 Horner House 1912 ADOLF LOOS
XIII, Nothartgasse 7 *U: Unter or Ober St Veit*
A splendidly cheap little house for Mme Helene Horner comprising two interlocking rectangles on a total groundplan of 11x10m. Main volume roofed in half-circular section, copper covered gives maximum usable space inside it, the other flat roofed as terrace. Walls and apertures entirely plain. Very little altered.

11 Lockerwiese Siedlung 1928-32
KARL SCHARTELMÜLLER
XIII, Faistauergasse, Engelhardtgasse, Wolkersbergenstrasse & Versorgungsheimstrasse *U: Hietzing then streetcar 60.*
At 643 dwellings this is less extensive than his similarly scaled no 36, of previous years, and strongly alternating pitched and flat roof elements divides the housing terraces with a more vertical emphasis. Curved roadways etc to give softness and variety to what still threatens to have super-block rather than cottage scale.

12 Steiner House 1910 ADOLF LOOS
XIII, St Veit-Gasse 10 *U: Unter St Veit*
Perhaps Loos' most famous villa, and first major one in Vienna

Steiner House, garden side, 1985 (photo Cooke)

following his numerous apartment interiors (see p 48). An utterly unornamented architecture of clean holes in plain stuccoed walls and probably the first private house in reinforced concrete. Central entrance up steps to small hall, with main dog-leg and circular service stairs off, through to living-dining room that spans whole width of rear. Essentially the same symmetry preserved on first floor, though attic, reached only by service stair, less formal, and has access to flat roof over rear. Front half originally roofed in quarter-circular section, copper plated - precursor of the half-circular section at Horner House of 1912. Now built out to a conventional front wall and pitched roof; famous garden elevation barely changed. Original clients: Hugo and Lilly Steiner.

13 Langer House 1900-1 JOSEF PLEČNIK
XIII, Beckgasse 30 *U: Unter St Veit*
Of Plečnik's small oeuvre in Vienna this is the only private house – something of a collaborative project with the client, master builder and local magistrate Karl Langer. A simple volume where decreasing public importance of internal spaces, L-R, is expressed in gradation from major bow-windows to small incised ones. The whole front patterned with stylised flower pattern in relief and Langer's trademark, a long-necked goose, naturalistically sculpted top R.

Langer House, facade detail, 1985 (photo Cooke)

14 Strasser House 1918-19 ADOLF LOOS
XIII, Kuppelwiesergasse 28 *U: Unter St Veit*
For Karl and Hilde Strasser. Remodelling of a ten-year-old house but the exterior more characteristically Loos' own than in Duschnitz or Mandl Houses, with half-barrel front roof as originally at Steiner House still preserved. Front elevation a layered relief of recessions, protrusions and excisions in squares. The entrance, left, into a small lobby turns immediately right into a well-lit entrance hall, whence one stair rises to the first floor, and another short flight descends into the comfortable lounge-hall running back to the garden. Off that, on the right of the house, pale gold and green onyx panelling of the dining room (both rooms illustrated by Kulka). The same material lines the library above the entrance, also preserved. Classic multi-directional stairs of his *Raumplan*.

15 Rufer House 1922 ADOLF LOOS
XIII, Schliessmanngasse 11
U: Unter St Veit or Braunschweiggasse
For Josef and Maria Rufer. The first pure and mature demonstration of Loos' *Raumplan* concept of free planning in three dimensions within a simple outer envelope (the second being the Moller house 1928). This one on square ground plan 10m x 10m, slightly taller than a cube, in which multiple levels and open interpenetrating spaces explore every corner and direction within the four storey volume (plans & interiors in Kulka). Free distribution of unlike windows on the cube's faces, develop the vocabulary first evident in Mandl house. Flat roof with strong cornice cut away for roof terrace at the back, where the volume is also cut away into a verandah. Kulka, as Loos' assistant, described this as 'the standard type for a house of this size that cannot be bettered'. Well preserved.

16 Scheu House 1912-13 ADOLF LOOS
XIII, La Roche-Gasse 3 *U: Braunschweiggasse*
The free-planning of Loos' emergent *Raumplan* concept applied in what is said to be the first terraced-house form in Central Europe; a halfway derivative of the apartment house made vertical, where the top-floor accommodation has its own street entrance, R, and the main house is entered at the side, L. Distinctive expression in the three-stepped front and rear elevations with slightly bolder fenestration to the garden. City building authorities originally insisted the street side be planted with creepers to clothe the nakedness, but now restored to Loos' original conception. Interiors were typical plain ceilings with dark panelling below, and interconnecting spaces with maximum fitted furniture. Original Clients were Dr Gustav and Mme Helene Scheu.

17 German High School 1930-1
SIEGFRIED THEISS & HANS JAKSCH
XIII, Wenzgasse 7 *U: Braunschweiggasse*
Totally uncompromising Modernist style of the early 1930s that is indeed international. Almost wholly glazed elevations between the r.c. frame; bare surfaces and steel doors etc classic of the genre.

18 House in Wenzgasse 1929-30
JOSEF FRANK & OSKAR WLACH
XIII, Wenzgasse 12 *U: Braunschweiggasse*
A large four storey house comparable in quality as well as manner to Loos' contemporary work (cf no 32). Fenestration clusters to the centre of a low rectangle, where a square protruding bay with bold circular window provides visual focus and key to the rest. Inside a programmatic demonstration of Frank's thesis that a house, like an organically grown, medieval town, comprises 'streets' and 'squares' and should explain itself with equivalent ease to the user.

19 Skywa-Primavesi House 1913-15 JOSEF HOFFMANN
XIII, Gloriettegasse 18 *U: Hietzing*
Resplendent house for the industrialist and politician Robert Primavesi and his second wife Josephine Skywa on large site with closely integrated landscaped garden. Built by Ast (see Ast House 1909-11), brick faced with golden stucco with concrete floors, and details as well as techniques similar to his own, though classical vocabulary of contemporaneous Austrian Werkbund Pavilions et al more dominant here over the picturesque composition. U-shaped plan entered at its centre from driveway R, rising into main panelled hall whence private wing runs L along street facade and rooms for their lavish entertaining progress ahead and left. Both sequences re-emerge onto a terrace over the garden, dominated by the half-circular bay or the library. See model p 34 where foreground greenhouse now destroyed. Pediment sculptures on the street facade by Anton Hanak. Numerous changes after war damage but they do not destroy the work; few original interiors remain. Now training centre for Austrian Labour Federation (ES cat 185).

20 Rosenhügel Garden Suburb 1921-6
HUGO MAYER & EMIL KRAUSE
XII, Defreggerstrasse, Endergass, Rosenhügelstrasse, Atzgerdorfer Strasse *U: Schönbrunn then bus 63A*
Again Mayer pioneers (cf no 33), here producing Vienna's most important cooperative *Siedlung* (housing settlement) of 559 dwellings. The first realisation of a totally 'new' lifestyle of self-management, with its own social centre and school, and full practical self-help including communal workshops and building materials purchase. Placid terraces of two storey housing dignified with vestigially classical flat-relief motifs over front doors etc.

21 Apartment House in Wattmanngasse 1914
ERNST LICHTBLAU
XIII, Wattmanngasse 29 *U: Hietzing*
Low-rise apartment building by Wagnerschule pupil who would later follow his fellow-student Schindler to the USA. Combines Modernist horizontal banding with majolica figurative decoration between windows – an interesting and attractive hybrid.

22 House in Auhofstrasse 1911-13 ROBERT OERLEY
XIII, Auhofstrasse 15 *U: Braunschweiggasse*
Major house for an industrialist in the unidactic free modern characteristic of this leader of the Hagenbund architects. Originally completely furnished by Oerley – a prolific furniture designer – but little now remains except the typically rather Arts and Crafts wood and copper detailing of main staircase and octagonal entrance vestibule. At this date (1911-12) Oerley was President of the Secession, which he joined in 1907 as traditional dominance

Oerley House, period view from the street. From Österreichische Werkkultur, 1916 (courtesy Durant).

INDEX OF ARCHITECTS

AICHINGER Hermann 1885-1962, 132 (1927-9)
BACH Theodor, 29(1897-9)
BASSET Walter, 127(1896-7)
BAUER Leopold 1872-1938, 67(1913-25), 45(1926), 129(1929-32)
BEHRENS Peter 1868-1940, 122(1924-5)
CHEDANNE Georges 1861-1940, 85 (1904-9)
DEININGER Wunibald 1879-1963, 56 (1905-8)
EHN Karl 1884-1959, 47(1925-7), 76(1926-30)
ENGELMANN Paul, 126(1926)

FABIANI Max 1865-1962, 125(1898-1900), 111(1900), 123(1909-10)
FERSTEL Heinrich von 1828-83, 105(1856-79), 92(1868-71), 104(1873-84)
FISCHL Karl 1871-?, 27(1904-5)
FLATTICH Wilhelm, 48(1870)
FRANK Josef 1885-1967, 38(1913-14), 30(1924-5), 122(1924-5), 18(1929-30), 7(1930), 50(1930-1)
GESSNER Frank 1879-?, 61(1905-7), 44(1907)
GESSNER Hubert 1871-1943, 61(1905-7), 44(1907), 59(1924-6), 128(1926-7), 79(1929-31)
GLASER Hans, 129(1929-32)
HACKHOFER Josef 1863-1917, 91(1903-6), 124(1903-7)

HAERDTL Oswald 1899-1959, 7(1930), 112(1932)
HANSEN Theophil 1813-91, 93(1864-7), 99(1868-73), 96(1871-7), 101(1873-83), 106 (1871-7)
HÄRING Hugo 1882-1958, 7(1930)
HASENAUER Carl von 1833-94, 97(1869-73), 98(1872-81), 102(1874-88)
HEGELE Max 1873-1945, 139(1907-10)
HETMANEK Alfons 1890-1962, 137 (1923-1928)
HOFFMANN Josef 1870-1956, 75(1900-1), 74(1901-2), 1(1903-5), 71(1906-7), 72(1909-11), 42(1912-13), 73(1912-13), 19(1913-15), 68(1923-5), 122(1924-5), 70(1924-5), 86(1928-32), 7(1930), 112(1932)

HOLZMEISTER Clemens 1886-?, 138 (1922), 43(1924-32), 7(1930)
HOPPE Emil 1876-1957, 133(1911-13), 28(1924-8)
JAKSCH Hans 1879-1970, 17(1930-1)
KASTINGER Herbert, 60(1928-30)
KASTNER Egon, 88(1929-31)
KAYM Frank 1891-1949, 137(19231928)
KOTĚRA Jan 1871-1923, 54(1914)
KREPP Karl, 134(1911-13)
KRIST Karl, 49(1927-30)
KULKA Heinrich 1900-71, 7(1930)
LASKE Oskar 1874-1951, 108(1902)
LEISCHNER Erich, 31(1928)
LICHTBLAU Ernst 1883-1963, 21(1914), 129(1929-32), 7(1930)

INDEX OF BUILDING TYPES

APARTMENT HOUSING Municipal or philanthropic: 48(1870), 29(1897-9), 35(1919-23), 68(1923-5), 51(1924), 31(1924-5), 122(1924-5), 59(1924-6), 28(1924-8), 47(1925-7), 45(1926), 128(1926-7), 76(1926-30), 131(1927-8), 132(1927-9), 49(1927-30), 86(1928-32), 129(1929-32), 50(1930-1), 121(1930-3). **Private:** 48(1870), 29(1897-9), 35(1919-23), 68(1923-5), 51(1924), 31(1924-5), 122(1924-5), 59(1924-6), 28(1924-8), 47(1925-7), 45(1926), 128(1926-7), 76(1926-30), 131(1927-8), 132(1927-9), 49(1927-30), 86(1928-32), 129(1929-32), 50(1930-1), 121(1930-3).

CHURCHES: 105(1856-79), 57(1895-8), 8(1905-7), 139(1907-10), 10(1910-13), 138(1922), 43(1924-32).

COMMERCIAL BUILDINGS (sometimes including apartments): 106(1871-7), 107(1882-4), 116(1890-1), 115(1893-5), 82(1899), 125(1898-1900), 111(1900), 108(1902), 118(1903-5), 61(1905-7), 56(1905-8), 117(1908), 110(1910), 114(1910-13), 109(1912), 113(1923), 112(1932).

EDUCATIONAL BUILDINGS: 104(1873-84), 123(1909-10), 17(1930-1).

ENGINEERING STRUCTURES: 37(1894-8), 46(1894-8), 77(1894-8), 127(1896-7), 91(1903-6), 124(1903-7), 120(1903-7), 79(1929-31).

HEALTH & RECREATIONAL BUILDINGS: 130(1898), 133(1911-13), 87(1923-6), 30(1928), 134(1929-31).

INDUSTRIAL BUILDINGS: 69(1888-92), 135(1911-13), 23(1917), 88(1929-31).

MEDICAL BUILDINGS: 1(1903-5), 64(1907-8), 24(1910-13).

PRIVATE HOUSES: 93(1864-7), 99(1868-72), 3(1886-8), 6(1899-1900), 89(1900-1), 13(1900-1), 25(1901-2), 4(1901), 74(1901-2), 84(1903), 72(1906-7), 44(1907), 73(1909-11), 41(1910-12), 5(1911-12), 22(1911-13), 10(1912), 16(1912-13), 42(1912-13), 71(1912-13), 2(1913-14), 38(1913-14), 19(1913-15), 54(1914), 55(1915-16), 53(1916-17), 14(1918-19), 15(1922), 40(1923-4), 70(1924-5), 126(1926), 32(1927-8), 18(1929-30).

PUBLIC BUILDINGS: 95(1861-9), 97(1869-73), 103(1872-83), 101(1873-83), 102(1874-88), 100(1875-81), 119(1904, 10), 85(1909), 67(1913-25), 60(1928-30), 17(1930-1).

SIEDLUNGEN (Low-rise suburban housing developments): 33(1919-20), 9(1921), 140(1921), 20(1921-6), 136(1923-7), 137(1923,28), 11(1928-32), 7(1930).

STADTBAHN STATIONS: 26(1894-6), 34(1896-7), 52(1896-8), 39(1896-8), 90(1897-8), 83(1898-9), 63(1898-9), 78(1900-1).

VISUAL ARTS BUILDINGS: 94(1865-8), 92(1868-71), 96(1871-7), 98(1872-81), 81(1897-8).

LIHOTZKY Margarete 1897-, 122(1924-5), 7(1930)
LOOS Adolf 1870-1933, 82(1899), 84(1903), 117(1908), 110(1910), 12(1910), 114(1910-13), 5(1911-12), 10(1912), 109(1912), 16(1912-13), 55(1915-16), 53(1922), 113(1923), 122(1924-5), 32(1927-8), 7(1930)
LURÇAT André 1894-1970, 7(1930)
MAYER Hugo, 33(1919-20), 20(1921-6)
MAYREDER Karl 1856-1935, 69(1888-92)
NADEL Otto, 87(1923-6)
NEUTRA Richard 1892-1970, 7(1930)
NÜLL Eduard van der 1812-68, 95(1861-9)
OERLEY Robert 1876-1945, 64(1907-8), 22(1911-13), 23(1917), 49(1927-30)
OHMANN Friedrich 1858-1927, 91(1903-6), 124(1903-7)
OLBRICH Joseph Maria 1867-1908, 26(1894-6 under Wagner), 81(1897-8), 130(1898), 6(1899-1900)
PERCO Rudolf, 121(1930-3)
PLEČNIK Josef 1872-1957, 13(1900-1), 25(1901-2), 62(1901-3), 118(1903-5), 10(1910-13)
PLISCHKE Ernst 1903-, 7(1930)
POLAK-HELLWIG Otto, 35(1919-23)
POPPOVITS Caesar, 51(1924)
RIETVELD Gerrit 1888-1964, 7(1930)
SCHARTELMULLER Karl, 136 (1923-7), 11(1928-32)
SCHEFFEL Karl, 129(1929-32)
SCHMALHOFER Karl, 87(1923-6)
SCHMID Friedrich von 1825-91, 103(1872-83)
SCHÖNTHAL Otto 1878-1961, 4(1900-1), 133(1911-13), 28(1924-8)
SCHWEITZER Erich-Otto, 135(1929-31)
SEMPER Gottfried 1803-79, 97(1869-73), 98(1872-81), 102(1874-88)
SICARDSBURG August von 1813-68, 95(1861-9)
SIMONY Leopold, 29(1897-9)
SOBOTKA Walter, 131(1927-8)
STEIGHOLZER Hermann, 60(1928-30)
STREIT Andreas, 116(1890-1)
STRNAD Oskar 1879-1935, 41(1910-12), 38(1913-14), 122(1924-5)
THEISS Siegfried 1882-1963, 17(1930-1)
WAAGE Fritz, 88(1929-31)
WAGNER Otto 1841-1918, 80(1877), 65(1880-3), 107(1882-4), 3(1886-8), 66(1888), 89(1890-1), 115(1893-5), 26(1894-6), 46(1894-8), 37(1894-8), 77(1894-8), 57(1895-8), 34(1896-7), 39(1896-8), 52(1896-8), 90(1897-8), 63(1898-9), 83(1898-9), 78(1900-1), 119(1904-6, 1910-12), 8(1905-7), 120(1906-7), 24(1910-13), 58(1909-10, 1912), 2(1913-14)
WEBER A., 94(1865-8)
WELZENBACHER Lois, 40(1923-4)
WIELEMANS Alexander 1843-1911, 100(1875-81)
WITTGENSTEIN Ludwig 1889-1951, 126(1926)
WLACH Oskar 1881-1963, 41(1910-12), 38(1913-14), 122(1924-5), 18(1929-30), 7(1930).

precipitated departure of the Klimt group. In front of the refined grey stone entrance porch here stand two vast blue and gold ceramic flower urns identical to those he installed astride the entrance to Olbrich's building, but still in superb condition (see inside back cover).

23 Zeiss Factory 1917 ROBERT OERLEY
XIV, Abbegasse 1   U: Lerchenfelderstrasse then bus 48A
A balanced piece of commercial architecture originally having a certain refinement of detailing suitable to its products. Five storeys with main length topped by mansard and oval windows, flanked by end 'towers' of angled corner. Now Phillips Factory.

24 Lupus Leprosy Sanatorium 1910-13 OTTO WAGNER
XVI, Montleartstrasse 37
U: Lerchenfelderstrasse then streetcar 46
Four storey rectangular building is now the central building (pavilion 24) of the Wilhelminen Hospital. Its interior has been rebuilt. Exterior rendered with light decorative emphasis from banding etc of blue tilework typical of Wagner's late work (cf Neustiftgasse apartment houses).

25 Adaptation of the Weidmann House 1901-2
JOSEF PLEČNIK & JOSEF CZASTKA
XIII, Hietzinger Hauptstrasse 6   U: Hietzing
Original single storey house adapted and enlarged for Josef Weidmann, fancy-goods manufacturer and eccentric antiques collector. On the street front only the second floor is fully intact, with putti playing around piers between attic windows under broad eaves. The first floor has lost some cartouches and the ground floor has been converted into shops. Original delicately rusticated facade here and rippling garden railings illustrated in Prelovšek; courtyard inside better preserved though orangery gone.

26 Hofpavilion Stadtbahn Station 1894-6
OTTO WAGNER
XIII, Schönbrunner Schlosstrasse   U: Hietzing
A one-off on the Wientallinie for private use of the Imperial family in nearby Schönbrunn Palace. Considered largely the work of Olbrich, then working in the office. A bald cupola, half Baroque, half Secessionist, over a square pavilion whose central waiting lounge was specially furnished and included a wall painting of Vienna from the air showing the whole Stadtbahn network for Imperial contemplation; entered from glazed iron porte-cochère. Now restored as a Stadtbahn museum.

27 Penzingerstrasse Apartment House 1904-5
KARL FISCHL
XIV, Penzingerstrasse 40   U: Hietzing
Best known remaining building by this pupil of Hasenauer and Wagner. Three main floors and attic; bold windows either side of angled and narrow central first floor bay-window. In a Jugendstil whose verticality and angularity also reflect Czech Cubism. Particularly good entrance and staircase remain.

28 Sandleiten Hof 1924-8
EMIL HOPPE, OTTO SCHÖNTHAL; SIEGFRIED THEISS, HANS JAKSCH.
XVI, Baumeistergasse, Metschgasse, Steinmüllergasse, Sandleitengasse   U: Schottentor then streetcar 2
Early example of the type, where vast overall size (Vienna's largest at 1,587 dwellings) is made a virtual 'town within the city' and given something of villa quality by low scale (four storeys plus dormers) and picturesque moments. Rosenackerstrasse divides Hoppe & Schönthal work to south from rest to north.

29 Jubilaumshäuser 1897-9
THEODOR BACH & LEOPOLD SIMONY
XVI, Madersperger strasse, Wernhardtstrasse, Gutraterplatz, Roseggerstrasse   U: Lerchenfelderstrasse then bus 48A
Four and five storey housing blocks with pitched roofs and bold fenestration around garden court, showing the 'hof' form in its 19th-century philanthropic variant. Housing for the poor erected by the Emperor Franz-Josef's Jubilee Fund formed in 1895. Well renovated.

30 Kongress Baths 1928 ERICH LEINSCHNER
XVI, Kongressplatz   U: Schottentor then streetcar 2
Public recreational facilities for the age of enlightenment. Swimming-baths, air and sunbathing in a temple to the healthbath culture of its time, in an equally programmatic simple, low rise architecture.

31 Wiedenhofer Hof 1924-5   JOSEF FRANK
XVII, Zeillergasse Pretschgogasse, Liebknechtgasse, Beringgasse
U: Schottentor then streetcar 2
Frank's skill with solid and void (in entrance and corner loggias) and overall handling of masses, makes architecture out of four storey blocks with simple fenestration. Originally dubbed

'Paprika-hof' for its warm red walls with bold white window frames (see also use of colour on no 50). Fifth floor within the attic zone added a new row of windows in 1953.

32 Moller House 1927-8   ADOLF LOOS
XVIII, Starkfriedgasse 19   U: Schottentor then streetcar 41
Back from Paris there is a Corbusian air to the front, whose classical symmetries give no warning of the dramatic spatial movements and interpretations of the multi-level Raumplan inside (see Rufer House 1922). Interior surfaces simpler than ever but still luxurious marble, timber etc of the highest quality. The cube promised by the front elevation is in fact terraced out progressively at each level of the rear to produce a section redolent of the Scheu's street elevation. Loos' last house in Vienna itself.

33 Housing Development in Schmelz 1919-20
HUGO MAYER
XV, Possingergasse, Gablenzgasse, Minciostrasse, Oeverseestrasse, Mareschplatz   U: Lerchenfelderstrasse then bus 48A
The first new municipal housing built after the War. Forty-one storey houses in four blocks, with small gardens in the courtyards, on former Schmelz parade ground. A second phase, of 1921-3, comprises simple two and three storey terraces given a picturesque air by pitched roofs, and dignified by a variety of 'pedimented' gables.

34 Schönbrunn Stadtbahn Station 1896-97
OTTO WAGNER
XII, Linke Wienzeile, Grünbergstrasse
U: this is now U-bahn's Schönbrunn Station
Typical example of the Wientallinie stations and lately restored. Pavilion form stylistically between Alser Strasse and Rossauer Länder as one would expect from its date of building; cf Stadtpark station.

35 Heimhof 1919-23   OTTO POLAK-HELLWIG
XV, Pilgerimgasse 22-24, Oeverseestrasse 25-9, Wurmsergasse, Johnstrasse   U: Volkstheater then streetcar 49
Charming first post-War example of collective living and for several years the only Vienna apartment complex with centralised catering. Also other facilities, all behind pleasingly urbane three storey classical facades.

36 Heilig-Geist-Church, Schmelz 1910-13
JOSEF PLEČNIK
XVI, Herbstrasse 82   U: Volkstheater then bus 48A
Vienna's first concrete church, for a suburban parish. Strippedbare classicism of 'doric' portico with lightly banded wall surfaces to square volume hanging behind. Massive paired hanging beams (concrete girders) from entrance to chancel create clerestory and lower 'aisles' and dramatic visual focus on altar, by Holub. Very different feel from Wagner's Steinhof church but from the beginning constantly invited that comparison. Crypt of facetted concrete beams and columns whose capitals and other surfaces originally covered in painted decoration and evoking medieval timberwork.

37 Richthausen Stadtbahn Bridge 1894-8
OTTO WAGNER
XVII, Richthausenstrasse & Hernalser Friedhof
U: Schottentor then streetcar 2
Took the Vorortelinie (Suburban Line) over the highway. Iron arch with delicate 'clip on' decorative details of cast-iron, between solid and very simply pilastered abutments.

38 Houses on Wilbrandtgasse 1913-14
JOSEF FRANK, OSKAR STRNAD & OSKAR WLACH
XIX, Wilbrandtgasse 3 & 11   U: Schottentor then streetcar 41
Two houses built from a planned group of four. Pre-date Loos' Moller House (no 32) by 15 years, but strikingly similar (if more

Street view, from Öst. Werkkultur, 1916 (courtesy Durant)

primitive) in flat, square entrance elevation with first-floor balcony all symmetrical, and terraced rear towards the garden.

39 Gersthof Stadtbahn Station 1896-98 OTTO WAGNER
XVIII, Gersthoferstrasse, Währingerstrasse & Gentzgasse
U: Schottentor then streetcar 40, 41
This station of the former Vorortelinie (Suburban Line), even more than the similarly classical Alser Strasse station of the Gurtellinie (Belt Line), speaks of the traditional 'grand railway station'. Its entrance between the columns of a protruding central archway.

40 Arnold House 1923-4   LOIS WELZENBACHER
XVIII, Sternwartestrasse 83   U: Schottentor then streetcar 41
Typical stripped, free-style classicism by this Tyrolean architect settled in Vienna. Four columned entrance 'portico' against a slightly curved plain stucco wall that follows the form of the site, and generally nice detailing.

41 House in Cobenzlgasse 1910-12
OSKAR STRNAD & OSKAR WLACH
XIX, Cobenzlgasse 71   U: Heiligenstadt then bus 38A
An original interpretation of the 'country' house, whose 'main' facade looks backwards over its garden from a portico on the top-floor piano nobile. Pitched roof and boldly framed windows are further links with the traditional housetype that belies the otherwise Loosian simplicity.

Side view, from Öst. Werkkultur, 1916 (courtesy Durant)

42 Kaasgraben Estate 1912-13   JOSEF HOFFMANN
XIX, Kaasgrabengasse 30/32, 36/38, and Suttingergasse 12/14, 16/18   U: Schottentor then streetcar 38
Four pairs of semi-detached villas, brick construction and tiled roofs, originally gleaming white stucco. In simplicity of volumes and materials marked contrast to earlier Hoffmann group on Wollergasse etc. Each different, though always compact plan, as for specific clients on initiative of the progressive music publisher Emil Hertzka and his feminist wife Yella who had Kaasgraben 32. Other owners were musical figures and progressive civil servants. Professional-class housing of highest standards with the innovation of hot-air heating. All somewhat altered but recognisable (ES cat 167).

43 Church of St Judas Thaddäus in der Krim 1924-32
CLEMENS HOLZMEISTER
XIX, Budinskygasse 19 U: Heiligenstadt then buses 10A and 35A
Less obviously 'expressive' than his no 138, though somewhat Expressionist street facade with two storey entrance arches, L & R, and tall slot in central tower. Stylistic cross between Loos and Swedish Modern. Nave extensions of 1957 not his plan.

44 Villa Gessner 1907   HUBERT & FRANZ GESSNER
XVIII, Sternwartestrasse 70   U: Schottentor then streetcar 41
Charming little suburban palazzo, low ground floor with piano nobile above having three flat-bay windows akin to those on their newly completed socialist printing house (no 61).

45 Vogelweid Hof 1926   LEOPOLD BAUER
XV, Hütteldorfer Strasse 2A, Sorbaitgasse, Wurzbachgasse
U: Margaretengürtel then streetcar 8
Among the most lastingly satisfactory of the 'hofs' of this period though small (127 apartments). Six stories with a very strong, smoothly patterned cornice, tall 'pilastered' attic, small windows in the solid wall and broad, boldly banded, round arcading at entrance – plus bas-reliefs and other decoration – give the elevations a welcoming and strongly Italian air.

46 Wienzeile Stadtbahn Bridge 1894-8 OTTO WAGNER
XII, Gumpendorfergürtel, Linke Wienzeile
U: Margaretengürtel
Takes the Gürtellinie (Belt Line) across the Wien River between Gumpendorferstrasse and Meidling Hauptstrasse stations. Simple braced girder bridge crosses its stone abutments at an angle in another example of Wagner's creation of architecture out of uncompromising engineering; cf contemporaneous Nussdorf locks.

47 Bebel Hof 1925-7 KARL EHN
XII, Steinbauergasse, Assmayergasse, Klährgasse, Längenfeldgasse   U: *Meidling Hauptstrasse*
Five to seven storey masses fragmented with towers, loggias, setbacks and street-level shops into quite pleasing composition. 331 apartments and full facilities around a single court by Ehn as City Architect.

48 Workers' Housing for the Southern Railway Co 1870
WILHELM FLATTICH
XII, Eichenstrasse   U: *Meidling Hauptstrasse*
A long range of four storey brick, its length broken by recessed entrance bays to stairs, decorated only by banding at sill levels. This company was the pioneer of workers' housing in Austria (cf also no 29 three decades later).

49 George Washington Hof 1927-30
ROBERT OERLEY & KARL KRIST
X,XII, Wienerbergerstrasse, Untere Meidlinger Strasse, Kastanienallee   U: *Meidling Hauptstrasse then bus 15A*
Typical large housing development of Red Vienna (1,085 apartments) but in even more determinedly anti-internationalist style than Oerley propagated against the Secessionists two decades earlier. Four blocks each of courtyard form. Eastern two (Birkenhof, Ahornhof) by Krist; western (Akazienhof, Ulmenhof) by Oerley. High-pitched roofs with dormers, picturesque composition and planting give a quasi-Garden City air.

50 Leopoldine Glökel Hof 1930-1 JOSEF FRANK
XII, Steinbauergasse, Gaudenzdorfergürtel, Herthergasse, Siebertgasse   U: *Margaretengürtel*
Perimeter planning round a large court. Blocks of the same planar simplicity as his villas, and equally dependent on placing and proportions of windows, balconies and dormers for its quality outside. Originally the staircases were individualised by different pastel washes of the stucco and alternating light and dark window surrounds (hence known as Aquarelle-hof), but this source of cheery atmosphere unfortunately not preserved in recent renovation.

51 Ludo Hartmann Hof 1924 CAESAR POPPOVITS
VIII, Albertgasse 13-15   U: *Rathaus*
An early and select little public housing development of 70 quite large (2-4 roomed) apartments for employees of the Rathaus (City Hall). Shopping arcade at ground level in the court where ceramic-clad columns emulate trunks of palm trees.

52 Alserstrasse Stadtbahn Station 1896-8
OTTO WAGNER
IX, XVII, Hernalser Hauptstrasse, Hernalsergürtel
U: *Schottentor then streetcar 2 or electric train to the station itself.*
Long facade of horizontal emphasis and regular though boldly Rationalist fenestration articulated, though no more, by a classical vocabulary. The entrance absorbed into the structural grid of the main elevation contrasts with its prominence at Gersthof on the same line.

53 Mandl House 1916-17 ADOLF LOOS
XIX, Blaasstrasse 8   U: *Friedensbrücke*
A conversion and enlargement (cf nearby Duschnitz house), transforming a villa into a piece of *Raumplan* on Loos' principles, that is reflected with new vigour in some dynamically asymmetrical fenestration. Main additions were to the south and east of original. Kulka illustrates a curved stair rising out of the galleried main hall.

54 Villa Lemberger 1914 JAN KOTĚRA
XIX, Grinzinger Allee 50   U: *Heiligenstadt then bus 38A*
Elements of Expressionist weight and dynamism and even, in the strange columns, of Czech Cubism, in a solid, stripped-classical mansion of two storeys. The only Vienna work of a prolific former Wagner pupil who by this time had created an equivalent to the Wagnerschule in the Academy of his native Prague.

55 Duschnitz House 1915-16 ADOLF LOOS
XIX, Weimarerstrasse 87   U: *Friedensbrücke*
Like the nearby Mandl House of the following year, a rebuilding and considerable enlargement of a pre-existing villa, here given a tall square tower on one side, now slightly altered, and sweeping pitched roofs. Interiors included finely parqueted music room with organ and marble walled dining room, and extensive use of glazed screen walls to assist flow of light and space. Kulka illustrates these spaces.

56 Handelsakademie 1905-8 WUNIBALD DEININGER
VIII, Hamerlingplatz 5-6   U: *Rathaus*
Business school for the Vienna merchant community, done soon after Deininger returned from his Rome Prize trip and three years in the Wagnerschule. Eclectic free-style detailing and typical flat-bay windows of that date (cf Fabiani & Gessners) within conventionally classical format of the late 19th-century commercial building. Doubtless the pretentiousness was just right for the clients.

57 Johanniskapelle c 1897 OTTO WAGNER
IX, Klammergasse, Wahringergürtel
U: *Schottentor then streetcar 40 or 41*
More street-furniture than architecture, recorded for completeness not intrinsic interest. A tiny cross-shaped form under a dome in plain classicism nicely enough detailed. Built in connection with the Gürtellinie of the Stadtbahn for reasons that remain obscure.

58 Neustiftgasse & Döblergasse Apartment Houses 1909-10, 1912 OTTO WAGNER
VII, Neustiftgasse 40 & Döblergasse 4   U: *Lerchenfelder Strasse*
Interesting comparison with the pair of similar size on Linke Wienzeile a decade earlier: their femininity and gratuitous if enjoyable decoration replaced by austere banding and crisp rectilinear geometry of Wagner's late style (cf his own Second Villa). Facades rendered with decoration in strips of black ceramic tiling. Bold typography of address panel and strong eaves are the only top-emphasis now. The blind panel with address above and window below on side elevation makes a

Wagner drawing, (Dream & Reality)

striking contrast with the similar element of the Universitätsstrasse block a decade earlier. Visual and functional demarcation of the lower two floors remains, though here rustication has become striped banding of black and white tiles. Ironwork etc is equally simple. Wagner himself had an apartment here (with the famous glass bath), which was as ever far more elaborate than the public exterior. Far from complete in its fittings, but restored and refurnished as a Wagner Museum. Hoffmann had his studio here, and also part of the Wiener Werkstätte (see above p 8).

59 Reumann Hof 1924-6 HUBERT GESSNER
V, Margaretengürtel 100-110, Siebenbrunnengasse, Brandmayergasse   U: *Margaretengürtel*
The first full realisation of the 'mass housing palace'. Hubert Gessner had joined Victor Adler's Social Democratic Party in 1918 (cf pp 26-7) and advanced its housing ideas enthusiastically (see also no 128). Here the strongly symmetrical planning of main and garden courts, monumental colonnaded entrance and attic etc, are a strong urban statement. Its eight to nine storeys embrace 480 dwellings, 11 studios, 19 commercial enterprises, plus workshops, central laundry and kindergarten.

60 Labour Exchange for the Timber- and Metal-working Industries 1928-30
HERMANN STIEGHOLZER & HERBERT KASTINGER
V, Emelgasse 2-4, Obere Amtshausgasse, Siebenbrunnenfeldgasse   U: *Margaretengürtel*
Massively cubic volume of largely 'unbroken wall-surfaces, relieved only by clustered vertical slots of fenestration from street to attic storeys. Rationalism of Behrens by whom Stiegholzer much influenced.

61 Vorwärts Building c.1905-7
HUBERT & FRANZ GESSNER
V, Rechte Wienzeile 97   U: *Pilgramgasse*
HQ for the Socialist party printing and publishing house 'Forwards' (cf note to no 59). Simple street elevation picks up levels of the classical building R, but typically reverses the emphasis to the top, with four flat-bay windows under a strong cornice above which the stepped fronton is framed by two upstanding worker figures. Converted to hotel.

62 Langer Apartment House 1901-3 JOSEF PLEČNIK
V, Rechte Wienzeile 68 & Steggasse 1   U: *Kettenbrückengasse*
Five and six storey block facing the canal, with and for the master builder Langer (cf Langer House 1900-1). Nice mixture of the highly geometrical, in window panels, striped rustication and balconies, with rippling curves at the eaves. The two themes combined in vertical banding on the fifth floor of the canal face, likewise in iron and plasterwork on the stairs.

63 Linke Wienzeile Apartment Houses 1898-9
OTTO WAGNER
VI, Linke Wienzeile 40, and corner of Linke Wienzeile 38 & Köstlergasse 1   U: *Kettenbrückengasse*
L, no 40, the 'Majolica House' over whose facade grows a swirling 'tree of life' of pink, green and blue tiles, mingling with sculpted lions heads and more architectural patterning below the deep and ornate cornice. Ground and first floor containing shops and commercial accommodation separated from four floors of apartments above by strong horizontal of iron balcony that stands on slender iron columns to form a linear verandah for the first floor. Big square of main elevation framed L & R with recessed corner loggias. Fine ironwork of the lift cages etc inside well preserved, and pleasant simplicity of detailing on the inner courtyard elevations. As in Rennweg et al, Wagner was developer here as well as architect. It is widely believed now that both buildings here were largely conceived and realised by students under his supervision.

The 'gilded building' R, no 38, has identical fenestration except for small attic lights, and the same horizontal balcony, but is terminated L & R by protruding pilasters. This is a corner building, whose main entrance is in the plainer facade on the side street at Köstlergasse 1. The ornate corner bay is semi-circular above over a polygonal base. Even more than the Majolica House this is an example of upward concentration of decoration, and on the corner bay, of putting the finest fenestration at the top (see discussion of Universitätsstrasse Apartment House, 1888). Alongside the open canal it works particularly well. Decoration of formalised fern and root motifs in gold with

banding, and oval bas-relief medallions of women's heads by Kolo Moser. The calling figures on the four corners of the roofline by Othmar Schimkowitz were originally gilded as well. In virtually every other detail these two buildings have recently been restored to their original states. (photo Cooke)

64 Auersperg Sanatorium 1907-8 ROBERT OERLEY
VIII, Auerspergstrasse 9   U: *Lerchenfelderstrasse*
Quite functional design of six storeys with strong horizontal emphasis of banding between windows. Originally a more distinctive roofscape of operating theatres using top light, and original glass around the main entrance, R, has gone. But good example of the middle road between Künstlerhaus and Secession represented by the Hagenbund of which Oerley was a founder member in 1900.

65 Stadiongasse Apartment Houses 1880-1, & 2-3
OTTO WAGNER
I, Stadiongasse 10 & 6-8   U: *Rathaus*
Much quieter facades than Schottenring building of 1877, though still strong horizontal divisions. No 10 of 1880-1 has banded rustication below with arched shop windows for the chemist and some corner emphasis. Nos 6-8 of 1882-3 without shop and even simpler. Street architecture to complement not compete with the vast Neo-Gothic and Neo-Renaissance complex of Rathaus nearing completion behind them. Another early Wagner apartment building (1884) in this district at Lobkowitzplatz.

66 Universitätsstrasse Apartment House 1888
OTTO WAGNER
I, Universitätsstrasse 12   U: *Schottentor*
Six storeys, two commercial and four residential, where top-emphasis of decoration, the scrollwork panels on corners and

bold windowless areas on the side elevation add up to a pleasurable balance between classicism and 'the new style'. This top-emphasis in decorative schema is said to have been conceived as much to increase the rentable value of otherwise less desirable top-floor apartments as to produce an aesthetic effect per se; Wagner made a new type out of balancing the two. Here the strength of this emphasis and femininity of decoration make this an important transitional work.

67 Nationalbank 1913-25 LEOPOLD BAUER
IX, Otto Wagner Platz 3 *U: Schottentor*
The major work from Bauer's period as Wagner's successor as Head of Academy School (1913-19), its construction interrupted by the War. Three storeys with strongly vertical emphasis and three 'attics' with receding roofs over solid ground floor, all in a very stripped Neo-Classicism. Could be the 'National Bank' in any country.

68 Klosehof Municipal Apartment Building 1923-5
JOSEF HOFFMANN
XIX, Philippovichgasse 1, also Werkmanngasse, Fickertgasse & Peezgasse *U: Friedensbrücke*
Hoffmann's contribution to the public housing programme launched in late 1923 in Vienna. All available resources on principle given to space rather than decoration. The latter restricted to some fluted wall surfaces and the 'classicising' of a main doorway with that and two Hanak sculptures, all now gone. The development occupies an entire street block with a courtyard that has another 'tower' of apartments in the centre. Some recessed balconies give relief to street facades, otherwise plain holes-in-walls (ES cat 255).

69 Zacherl Factory 1888-92 KARL MAYREDER
XIX, Nusswaldgasse 14 *U: Heiligenstadt*
The architect, a fan of Stübben, became Chief of Vienna's Planning Dept two years later, in 1894, and with his engineer brothers, had a big influence on the city's development. Here a very strange mixture of Gothic with Persian ceramic details and facing, for an insecticide factory whose main raw materials came from Persia (*cf* Plečnik no 111).

70 Knips House 1924-5 JOSEF HOFFMANN
XIX, Nusswaldgasse 22 *U: Heiligenstadt*
Not a large house but sumptuous, and well preserved today. Sonja Knips, born Baroness Potier des Echelles, was a friend and patron of Secessionists since her youth. Klimt's 1898 portrait of her had been his breakthrough from naturalism towards more planar abstraction (see p 50, R), and was exhibited at the 2nd Secession exhibition. Hoffmann did interiors for their city-centre apartment in 1903 and 1915-16 of which some were transferred here, where original design dates from 1919. Main house like a six-bayed Georgian house, extended R into an L-shaped wing of service accommodation broken near its angle by a driveway. Main windows of the house banded in rich relief – almost the only external decoration. Internally, one of Hoffmann's most subtle and rich colour schemes, changing from room to room. Fabrics by Dagobert Peche and colour schemes of plasterwork etc by another prized student, Christa Ehrlich. Built by Ast and in superb condition still (ES cat 265). Hoffmann's last great Viennese villa.

71 Bernatzik House 1912-13 JOSEF HOFFMANN
XIX, Springsiedelgasse 28 *U: Heiligenstadt*
A free standing villa on square plan with rather vertical proportions; stuccoed brick, tiled roof as in Kaasgraben group and many similar features, including fluted surface to second storey. Not as closely connected to its gardens as most Hoffmann houses. Furnished by him, and in all respects well preserved (ES cat 168). Client was a law professor whose son and daughter had close involvement with Secession and Wiener Werkstätte.

72 Second Moll House 1906-7 JOSEF HOFFMANN
XIX, Wollergasse 10 *U: Heiligenstadt*
Another relatively modest suburban villa in this select area, for Carl Moll (interior painting by Moll p 45). U-shaped plan around central stair hall that penetrates full height of house to studio in attic. Kitchen at ground floor of tower-like element, R of front; big loggia connects to garden R at rear. Not just windows (see Purkersdorf) but gutter at eaves et al are banded in chequered tiles, here black and white. Restored to near original appearance (ES cat 112).

73 Ast House 1909-11 JOSEF HOFFMANN
XIX, Steinfeldgasse 2 & Wollergasse 12 *U: Heiligenstadt*
Last and largest of Hoffmann's group here, standing between Spitzer and Moll-2. For Eduard Ast, the Austrian pioneer of reinforced concrete with whom Hoffmann worked increasingly consistently and already did Kunstschau pavilions (see p 42), Moll-2 et al. Comparable as an integrated design and furnishing job to the Stoclet, though more relaxed, and to the later Skywa-Primavesi house which Ast would also construct. Large square villa raised imperiously above the street, extending outwards in loggia terraces to luxuriant grounds. Hovers stylistically between the classicism emergent in the Kunstschau and the former free-style, in particular in the elevations. Fluted vertical panels of stuccoed concrete give a trabeated air whilst luxuriant banding and 'cushions' of stylised plant forms demonstrate the possibilities of the new encrustation technique developed by Ast. A little changed, especially inside, but essentials all there.

Ast House, detail of garden front, from the first Yearbook of the German Werkbund, *1912 (courtesy Durant) cf p 67.*

74 Spitzer House 1901-2 JOSEF HOFFMANN
XIX, Steinfeldgasse 4 *U: Heiligenstadt*
For Dr Friedrich Spitzer. Last of the group of four early Hoffmann houses here (see no 75). Similar in style and type, here top accommodation is a study, originally outstanding in grey and white. Dining and music rooms initially contained the interiors Olbrich had done for his city apartment – noted at the time to be a little incongruous here. Little now remains of original interiors, but exterior well preserved if overgrown by creeper (ES cat 63).

Detail of the Spitzer House, R, with the Moser House, L, from The Studio, *1904.*

75 Moll & Moser Houses 1900-1 JOSEF HOFFMANN
XIX, Steinfeldgasse 8 & 6 *U: Heiligenstadt*
Semi-detached pair, the larger, L on street, for Carl Moll, the smaller, R, for Kolo Moser. First houses of the group in this area initially conceived by Olbrich (see his Bahr House 1899). Domestic comfort very much on the English model with high-pitched roof above a fake half-timbering applied to stuccoed brick. Both have studios and masterbedrooms at the top, commanding superb views. Plans organised around central stair from a living-hall, with kitchens, staff, etc, in half-basement. Dynamic outline and variety of textures give enlarged sense of scale. Great attention to use of exterior space for each owner's needs. Moll house altered; his painting of the terrace, p 34 above and an interior, p 44. Moser house barely recognisable (ES cats 52, 53). Neighbouring Wollergasse 8, now unrecognisable, was next of the group, of same date, organisation and style, for Dr Hugo Henneberg, a Secession supporter and patron of Mackintosh (ES cat 54).

76 Karl-Marx Hof & Svoboda Hof 1926-30 KARL EHN
XIX, Heiligenstadter Strasse 82-92, Grinzinger Strasse & Boschstrasse *U: Heiligenstadt*
Most famous of the super-block 'hofs', and one kilometer in total building length. One of the largest elements of 'the Proletariat's Ringstrasse' (see pp 61-3). The 'reality' motif of Hollein's Künstlerhaus exterior for the exhibition derived from the distinctive repeat-element of its seven storey elevations. 1,382 apartments with full communal facilities around one main and two garden courts. Scale and monumentality from the outer elevational plane that rises from vast low arches to form the rhythm of balconies and towers.

77 Nussdorf Canal Lock 1894-8 OTTO WAGNER
XIX, near Nussdorfer Platz *U: Heiligenstadt*
Locks and remodelling of offices for the Danube Regulation Commission so that the Danube canal could be used as a winter harbour. Synthesis of engineering with architectural elements into a model element of the functioning city landscape. Lock and abutments substantially rebuilt in early 1970s.

78 Rossauer Lände Stadtbahn Station 1900-1
OTTO WAGNER
II, IX, Rossauer Lände Canal Embankment
U: this is now U-bahn's Rossauer Lände station
On the Danube Canal Line. Masterly resolution of movements and different elevational axes at the three levels of upper street, trains and canalside path below. Fine ironwork.

79 Augartenbrücke 1929-31 HUBERT GESSNER
II, IX, Donaukanal *U: Schottenring*
Architectural detailing of a bridge built by engineers Waagner-Biro, with pleasant Art Deco air in places.

80 Schottenring Apartment House 1877
OTTO WAGNER
I, Schottenring 23 *U: Schottenring*
Urbane and handsome proportioning of a square facade with strong horizontal divisions, rising from two rusticated floors, two *bel étages* with trompe l'oeil facetted surface to strong attic and cornice; arched central doorway. A top emphasis and thrusting terminal pilasters L & R are already prescient of dynamic compositional modes in future, though the language here is firmly Renaissance classicism.

81 Secession Building 1897-8 JOSEPH MARIA OLBRICH
I, Friedrichstrasse 12 *U: Karlsplatz*
The filigree dome has now been regilded and the open flexible organisation so praised in the original interior recreated as part of its restoration, by Krischanitz and Kapfinger, 1986, for a gallery of contemporary art. Hermann Bahr eulogised over its functionality as ' a space designed to allow works of art to produce the greatest possible effect'. Olbrich insisted its origins were in 'pure sublime feeling'. Undoubtedly a brilliant synthesis of the two, though exterior surfaces of solid main volumes never as decorated as even Olbrich's final scheme intended. Erected in six months, to give the Secessionists their own permanent gallery. In the early years its movable panel system fully exploited to 'redesign' the space several times a year for major shows. A new basement houses Klimt's Beethoven Frieze. For building plan see p 7, and on 1902 'Beethoven' show, see pp 4-7 and 54-57.

82 Café Museum 1899 ADOLF LOOS
I, Friedrichstrasse/ Operngasse corner *U: Karlsplatz*
L-shaped cafe along two street frontages entered at corner and in the two sides; spacious almost undecorated interior with low-arched ceiling. All furniture etc by Loos (table and chair, see p 44), the polished mahogany and inlaid brass of bar fittings etc perhaps a theme absorbed from his stay in England three years before. Location near Academy of Arts, Technical University and Secession building immediately made it a meeting place of artists. Only facade remains and that far from complete.

83 Karlsplatz Stadtbahn Station 1898-9
OTTO WAGNER
I, on Karlsplatz opposite the Künstlerhaus *U: Karlsplatz*
Originally the two pavilions were entrances, on opposite sides of the street, to separate platforms of the Wientallinie below. The original Ferdinandsbrücke station, later Schwedenplatz, was the only other one of this type. Interesting prefabricated construction of 2cm thick marble sheet and 5cm stucco sheets with 3cm cavity between cast iron frames has facilitated their movement, in replanning of Karlsplatz, to be outpavilions for coffee and Wagner of the Künstlerhaus. Barrel vaulted central roofs a harmonious linear version of the Karlskirche cupola to which they originally stood very close. Now again sparkling in gold, white and green.

84 Loos' Apartment 1903 ADOLF LOOS
I, Bösendorferstrasse 8, now in Historisches Museum, Lothringerstrasse *U: Karlsplatz*
Living room from the home Loos set up with his first wife Lina, formerly on the 5th floor in Bösendorfer 8 (then Giselastrasse), now exhibited in slightly altered form in Museum in next street. Inglenook fireplace with tall hood, exposed brickwork, timbered ceiling, rug etc suggest again (*cf* no 82) influence of English travels in late 1890s.

85 French Embassy 1909 GEORGES CHEDANNE
IV, Technikerstrasse 2   U: Karlsplatz
Bulky building of complex form in a combination of Art Nouveau and classicism typical of Chedanne, who is often compared to François Jourdain. Consciously transplanting the stonework, metal roof and balconies of the Parisian streetscape in a form of 'official Art Nouveau'.

86 Laxenburgerstrasse Apartments 1928-32
JOSEF HOFFMANN
X, Laxenburgerstrasse 94   'U: Reumannplatz
332 flats for the City Council in a five storey perimeter development giving spacious central court with vehicle access and stairs off. Fairly accurate impression of original still inside court, but street facades have been stripped of their stucco stripes and open iron balconies have been filled in. Otherwise in good condition (ES cat 307).

87 Amalienbad 1923-6
OTTO NADEL, KARL SCHMALHOFER
X, Reumannplatz 9   U: Reumannplatz
Extraordinary symmetrical cubic pile, four storeys stepping back to a central clocktower of about ten storeys, under Schmalhofer as City Architect. A variation on the health theme of no 30, capable of accommodating 1,300 people in its vast swimming pool, solarium with sliding glass roof etc. Superbly appointed as 'Europe's largest spa', and steambath et al currently being restored.

88 Transformer Station 1929-31
EGON KASTNER & FRITZ WAAGE
X, Humboldtgasse 1-5, Sonnwendgasse   U: Keplerplatz
Two and five storey forms rising above a single storey base in a piece of Constructivist-inspired industrial architecture that is rare, if not unique, in Vienna.

89 Wagner's Town House 1890-1   OTTO WAGNER
III, Rennweg 3   U: Karlsplatz
Centre and most ornate of the trio, nos 1, 3 & 5 (the latter being also Auenbruggegasse 2) built by Wagner as architect and developer. No 1 much altered. No 3 for himself has delicately delineated five-bay facade with two balconied loggias for the bel étage at the first floor level framing a grand three-bayed central living room. His office behind the equivalent windows at street level. Later the Hoyos House, now Embassy of Yugoslavia.

90 Stadtpark Stadtbahn Station 1897-98
OTTO WAGNER
I, Lothringerstrasse, Johannesgasse, Stadtpark   U: Stadtpark
Follows the general scheme of Wientallinie stations as seen in Schönbrunn, extended into a screen wall and lamp 'column' L by Ohmann. Both have a slightly oriental air in the build-up of low-pitched roofs over square plans. Also lately restored and now a U-bahn station.

91 River Wien Embankment 1903-6
FRIEDRICH OHMANN & JOSEF HACKHOFER
I, Stadtpark-Johannesgasse   U: Stadtpark
Waterside landscaping of corner pavilions and embankment promenades with Stadtpark. In a felicitous mixture of Secession and Neo-Baroque that goes well with Wagner's station (no 90). Both architects were pupils of König – Ohmann also of Ferstel, and at this date an Academy Professor.

Buildings of the Ringstrasse (pp 26, 28-9)

92 Museum of Art and Industry 1868-71
HEINRICH VON FERSTEL
I, Stubenring 5   U: Landstrasse
Modest five-bayed Neo-Renaissance palazzo with wings, now the Museum of Applied Arts.

93 Palace of Archduke Wilhelm 1864-7
THEOPHIL HANSEN
I, Parkring 8   U: Landstrasse or Stadtpark
Splendid residence in confident Neo-Renaissance style. Roof zone recently altered.

94 Künstlerhaus 1865-8   A WEBER
I, Karlsplatz 5   U: Karlsplatz
For the private exhibition society of this name founded in 1861 by von Sicardsburg, from which the Secessionists broke away in protest in 1897 and built themselves Olbrich's no 81. Site of Dream and Reality exhibition: see pp 15-16.

95 State Opera House 1861-9
A VON SICARDSBURG & E VAN DER NÜLL
I, Opernring 2   U: Karlsplatz
Neo-Renaissance with a light touch and bold five-arched grand loggia. Reconstructed after destruction in last War.

96 Academy of Fine Art 1871-7
THEOPHIL HANSEN
I, Schillerplatz 3   U: Karlsplatz or Mariahilferstrasse
Neo-Renaissance with mass-produced terracotta decoration.

97 New Hofburg 1869-73
GOTTFRIED SEMPER, CARL VON HASENAUER et al
I, Hofburg, Heldenplatz   U: Mariahilferstrasse
Great half-round court with arcade of paired columns but only half the intended project realised.

98 Art Historical Museum 1872-81
GOTTFRIED SEMPER then CARL VON HASENAUER
I, Burgring 5   U: Mariahilferstrasse
Long Neo-Renaissance pile with central cupola, facing similar Natural History Museum across the platz.

99 Epstein Palace 1868-72
THEOPHIL HANSEN
I, Dr Karl Renner Ring 1   U: Volkstheater
Four storey Neo-Renaissance palazzo with rich attic decoration and bold detailing. Now Stadtschulrat (Schools Council). Otto Wagner was executive architect in the office, his early Bellariastrasse 4, is round the corner.

100 Palace of Justice 1875-81
ALEXANDER WIELEMANS
I, Museum Strasse   U: Volkstheater or Lerchenfelderstrasse
Competition of 1874 won by this pupil of von Sicardsburg and van der Nüll. Fine piece of late classicism. Bits destroyed in 1927 riots redone in other styles.

101 Parliament Buildings 1873-83
THEOPHIL HANSEN
I, Dr Karl Renner Ring 3   U: Lerchenfelderstrasse
Designed 1871; magnificent Greek Revival by the man widely considered Europe's last great classicist.

102 Burgtheater 1874-88
GOTTFRIED SEMPER & C VON HASENAUER
I, Dr Karl Lueger Ring   U: Rathaus
Free Neo-Renaissance with fine apsidal end onto Ring.

103 New Town Hall (Rathaus) 1872-83
FRIEDRICH VON SCHMIDT
I, Rathausplatz 1, Felderstrasse, Friedrich-Schmidtplatz, Lichtenfeldgasse   U: Rathaus
Extensive and extraordinary combination of Neo-Gothic and Neo-Renaissance.

104 New University Buildings 1873-84
HEINRICH VON FERSTEL
I, Dr Karl Lueger Ring 1   U: Schottentor
Ferstel's most famous work: a complex of pavilions and galleries in free Neo-Renaissance.

105 Votive Church 1856-79   HEINRICH VON FERSTEL
IX, Rooseveltplatz   U: Schottentor
Essentially Neo-Gothic. Ferstel won the competition. His first solo project that made his reputation.

106 Bours 1871-7   THEOPHIL HANSEN
I, Schottenring 16   U: Schottentor
Cubic volumes and Neo-Renaissance detailing.

Inside the Ringstrasse

107 Länderbank Building 1882-4   OTTO WAGNER
I, Hohenstaufengasse 3   U: Schottentor
A plain and clean-cut classical elevation leads to subtle handling of angled axis on the site behind through a circular hallway. Thence to an ingenious half-round banking hall developed from his Deposit and Credit Bank competition scheme of 1880 with glazed ceiling, above which a two storey horseshoe of offices around a broad lightwell also roofed in glass. Resplendent classicism in public interiors and a simplicity of timber and glass interiors in offices that anticipates his Rationalist work.

108 Engel's Chemist Shop 1902   OSKAR LASKE
I, Bognergasse 9   U: Stephansplatz
An agreeable bit of Art Nouveau comprising two angels and a floral panel with birds around a low-arched street entrance and rectangular window above. By a pupil of Wagner at the Academy whose main career was to be in graphics.

109 Manz Bookshop Facade 1912   ADOLF LOOS
I, Kohlmarkt 16   U: Stephansplatz
Classic Loos shopfront of recessed central entrance, here with glazed and top-lit ceiling, display windows L & R, all faced in dark marble with the simplest lettering of shop name and contents. Windows renovated in connection with recent redesign of interior.

110 Loos Building (Michaelerplatz Building) 1910
ADOLF LOOS
I, Michaelerplatz 3   U: Stephansplatz
Loos' first and principle non-domestic building and demonstration of the theories expounded in his earlier critiques, eg in Ver Sacrum, of public building of the Ringstrasse era and type. On the scandal caused by it, and for exterior and model, see pp.46-7. As already characteristic of Wagner's work and others of older generation, lower two floors of commercial accommodation (here the men's outfitters Goldman & Salatsch) given clear visual demarcation from the apartment floors above. G & S accommodation and entrance lobbies etc were finished with great simplicity in luxurious materials: marbles selected in Greece by Loos – green-grey on the street and pinkish inside – fine polished hardwoods, highest quality metal and glass fittings etc. A cosmopolitan air from this truth-to-materials effect that could be Chicago or London, though extreme simplicity is Loos' own. The shop went bankrupt in 1925/6, and interior almost entirely destroyed, though well recorded in photographs.

111 Artaria Building 1900   MAX FABIANI
I, Kohlmarkt 9   U: Stephansplatz
Apartment and commercial building for publishers. Typically simple piers and vitrines at street level. Above that a softer elevation than for his just-previous no 125, thanks to rippling, somewhat Mackintosh-like low-relief bay-windows – three on each of four upper floors – which became a widespread motif among his generation of Wagnerschule.

112 Altmann & Kühne Sweetshop 1932
JOSEF HOFFMANN & OSWALD HAERDTL
I, Graben 30   U: Stephansplatz
A late example but similar to that of 1928 which is destroyed. Fascia as deep as window below, white with shop name in simple sans-serif face. Fine materials applied to commerce without the heaviness of Loos' earlier schemes: glass, metals and highly polished wood in the interior, mostly well preserved (ES cat 338).

113 Leschka Outfitters Shop 1923
ADOLF LOOS
I, Graben 16   U: Stephansplatz
A very narrow street frontage that combines elements of the Kniže and Manz shopfronts but asymmetrically, having only room for one large display window L of door and a small one R. The usual marble, glass and bronze, though interior completely altered.

114 Kniže Outfitters Shop 1910-13
ADOLF LOOS
I, Graben 13   U: Stephansplatz
Tiny street frontage of marble, bronze and glass leads to narrow ground-floor salesroom entirely walled with display and storage in natural materials, thence by small stair to spacious first-floor sales and fitting rooms with the air of a country-house dressing room, in leather, brass, mahogany etc. Typography on the street frontage has a less imperial air than original, but otherwise this is the best preserved of accessible Loos interiors. Timeless quality and simplicity.

115 Anker Building 1893-5   OTTO WAGNER
I, Graben 10 & Spiegelgasse 2   U: Stephansplatz
For the Anchor Insurance Co. Makes an interesting comparison with Streit's far more ornate Equitable Building of 1890-1 on a similar site, also with lower floors for commerce clearly demarcated on facade from apartment floors above (no 116). In both cases central three bays of the main end elevation grouped, and separated from single bays L & R by pilasters, but Wagner's treatment is strongly cubic. Likewise the domed mansard end of the earlier scheme has become usable space of fully developed penthouse, conceived as his own studio but used by a photographer, and now by the painter Hundertwasser.

116 Equitable Building 1890-1   ANDREAS STREIT
I, Stock-im-Eisen-Platz 3-4   U: Stephansplatz
Interesting historical prototype for nearby no 115 by Wagner. Typical commercial architecture of its period for the New York life-assurance company, in a germanic Neo-Baroque.

117 American Bar 1908   ADOLF LOOS
I, Kärntner Durchgang   U: Stephansplatz
Also called the Kärnter Bar. Minute space 4.5 x 6.5m on plan, panelled and mirrored inside by Loos to seem far larger. A sensation at the time and still showpiece, though at time of writing very run down, and awaits replacement of facade with exhibition reconstruction (see pp 48-9).

118 Zacherl Building 1903-5
JOSEF PLEČNIK
I, Bauernmarkt-Brandstätte 6 & Wildpretmarkt 2-4
U: Stephansplatz
Commercial accommodation for the industrial firm of Johann Evangelist Zacherl, with apartments above. Their factory of 1888 by Mayreder (no 69) was in broad Gothic, and there is something redolent of that in the angling of lower and attic windows here, the vertical emphases, the strongly three-dimensional sculpture at attic and in single free-standing figure when contemporaneous work (and his own preliminary projects here) were accentuating flatness with surface decoration. The corner curve was a feature of all designs for the site, including rival ones by Schönthal, but this smooth constructive treatment of Plečnik's final design gives it maximum tension.

119 Post Office Savings Bank 1904-6, (1910-12)
OTTO WAGNER
I, Georg Coch Platz 2   U: Schwedenplatz
One of the masterpieces of integrated Rationalist design in this period, with every technical detail, from hot-air pipes to furniture, incorporated into the overall formal as well as functional schema. See colour photos p 20. First-prize winner in competition. Street facades that are urbane and unassertive lead to magnificent use of natural materials in the dramatic interiors: aluminium, glass, ceramics as well as natural stones and timbers. Much of Wagner's specially designed original furniture is still in use in both public spaces and offices (see p 45). Back part dates from 1910-12.

Outside the Ringstrasse – East

120 Kaiserbad Sluice Building 1906-7   OTTO WAGNER
II, Obere Donaustrasse near no 26, at the Canal
U: Schottenring
See colour photo p 24 above. Recalls his Rossauer Lände Stadtbahn Station of 1900-1 in the layered, multi-axial handling of canalside site. Original dam structure across the canal now gone, but moving gantry with engine for lifting sluices originally ran in and out along the top of the watergates from the large doors at towpath level, whilst controller operated from vantage point of projecting cabin above. Main wall facing is white marble slabs bolted on (cf Post Office Savings Bank) with rippling wave pattern in white on deep blue tiles at eaves level forming an enjoyably maritime detail.

121 Housing Complex at Friedrich Engels Platz 1930-3
RUDOLF PERCO
XX, Friedrich Engels Platz, Wehlistrasse, Leystrasse, Forsthausgasse, Kapaunplatz   U: Heiligenstadt
Interesting comparison with two other developments of this scale (1,467 apartments) such as Sandleiten Hof (no 28) or Karl-Marx (no 76). Vast open court surrounded by eight storeys of uniform fenestration with clustered minimal balconies and a vertical rhythm of stairtowers. None of the social urgency of 76, or the oppressiveness, but does make one ask if it has to be so anonymous.

122 Winarsky Hof & Otto Haas Hof 1924-5
BEHRENS, FRANK, HOFFMANN, LIHOTZKY, LOOS, STRNAD & WLACH
XX, Stromstrasse 36-38, also Winarskystrasse, Durchlaufstrasse & Pasettistrasse   U: Heiligenstadt
Early public housing complex under the programme launched in autumn 1923. Here six storeys in several large courtyards totalling 807 apartments on usual staircase access. Minor differences between work of different architects, viz: staircases 15, 24, 25, 28-32 by Behrens, 1-14, 26, 27 totalling 76 apts by Hoffmann (ES cat 264); 16-23 by Frank, Strnad & Wlach, all in Winarsky Hof. Others did Otto Haas Hof. All in good condition.

123 Urania 1909-10   MAX FABIANI
I, Uraniastrasse I   U: Schwedenplatz
Extraordinary building of five storeys on elliptical plan whose seven storey tower, bold free classicism and riverside promontory position gives it the air of a bulky harbour lighthouse. Conceived by its first president Ludwig Koessler as a 'palace for popular education'. A rich mix of accommodation includes large auditoria, within a complex spatial system worthy of Loos. Fabiani's intermediate position between Historicism and Secession, evidenced here, made him ideal as architectural adviser to the ill-fated heir to the throne Franz-Ferdinand. Building messed around after last War, but essentials remain.

124 Zollamtsteg 1903-7
FRIEDRICH OHMANN & JOSEF HACKHOFER
I, III, Wiental, Vordere Zollamtsstrasse   U: Landstrasse
Parabolic arch in iron above a diagonal bridge below, where the Stadtbahn's Wientallinie and Donaukanallinie intersect and cross the River Wien. More florid ornament than Wagner's nos 37 or 46, but similarly vigorous contribution to the townscape (see also no 91).

125 Portois & Fix Building 1898-1900   MAX FABIANI
III, Ungargasse 59-61   U: Stadtpark
For the furniture company who made many Wiener Werkstätte pieces like the Moser dining room suite of 1900 on p 45 above. Follows the injunction of his master Wagner to use colour abstractly, in geometrical polychrome tilework of the main elevation. Otherwise typical Wagnerschule commercial building with two floors, shop etc, highly glazed, under solid walls of apartments over.

126 Wittgenstein House 1926
LUDWIG WITTGENSTEIN & PAUL ENGELMANN
III, Kundmanngasse 19   U: Landstrasse
Uncompromising Modernism whose character owes as much to the client's philosophical theories, in proportions of spaces and apertures etc, as to the overall rational style and constructive details. Built while Wittgenstein was teaching in Austria before resuming philosophical research in Cambridge in 1929-30.

127 Riesenrad (Giant Ferris-wheel) 1896-7
WALTER BASSET & Engr. HITCHENS
II, Volksrater   U: Praterstern
Spectacular and at the time controversial structure 67m high, erected by English engineers and still functioning for your delight. You saw it first in The Third Man.

Karl Seitz Hof, street view (courtesy Czech)

128 Karl Seitz Hof 1926-7   HUBERT GESSNER
XXI, Jedleseer Strasse 66-94, Voltagasse, Bunsengasse, Dunantgasse, Edisongasse   Schnellbahn: Floridsdorf then bus 33B
'Mass housing palace' (cf no 59) on truly monumental scale with 1,173 dwellings. Great curved entrance block on Jedleseer Street, with massive arch and clocktower over, and integration into the street axes through vistas and curves around it, makes it a powerful piece of urbanism rather than just architecture. Some nice detailing of Art Deco flavour around entrances inside.

Paul Speiser Hof, inside Lichtblau court (courtesy Czech)

129 Paul Speiser Hof 1929-32
HANS GLASER, KARL SCHEFFEL; ERNST LICHTBLAU: LEOPOLD BAUER
XXI, Franklinstrasse, Bodenstedtgasse, Grossmannplatz, Freytaggasse   Schnellbahn:. Floridsdorf
Effectively three developments: by Glaser & Scheffel in '29-30, Lichtblau in '30-1 & Bauer in '31-2, so mixing their different architectures. Most convincing is perhaps Lichtblau's, to the north: white with red roofs and bold rectangles of glazing in four storey loggia-towers on street that repeat at courtyard level inside.

130 Civil Servants' Cycling Club 1898
JOSEPH MARIA OLBRICH
II, Rustenschacher Allee 7   U: Praterstern then bus 80A
Now the Sportclub Schwarz-Blau. A substantially unaltered building to which Christian Nebehay has refocused attention. Modest and single storey, with symmetrical main elevation redolent of his master Wagner's comtemporaneous designs for Wientallinie Stadtbahn stations at Schönbrunn and especially Stadtpark. A soft centre, here spanned by low-curving archway and other wood work, between two hard ends of masonry each with a single incised window. Appropriate and charming.

131 Klopsteinplatz Housing Complex 1927-8
WALTER SOBOTKA
III, Klopsteinplatz 6 & Schrottgasse 10-12
U: Landstrasse then streetcar T
A relatively small development (66 apartments) where the main volumetric effect comes from handling of the loggias and the single storey 'skirt' of large-windowed kindergarten at g.l.

132 Rabenhof 1927-9
HEINRICH SCHMID & HERMANN AICHINGER
III, Baumgasse 29-41, Rabengasse, Lustgasse, St Nikolas Platz, Hainburger Strasse   U: Landstrasse then streetcar J
One of the super-large complexes (1,109 dwellings) with full communal facilities. Somewhat picturesque planning around a series of courts, and a lot of Expressionist detailing, give a flavour more National-Romantic than Modernist.

133 Trotting Racetrack Grandstand 1911-13
EMIL HOPPE & OTTO SCHÖNTHAL
II, Prater, Trabenstrasse, Südportalstrasse
U: Praterstern then streetcar I
Handsome slender reinforced concrete construction built just after the two left Wagner's office in 1910 to set up independently. Later modifications have slightly detracted from the purity of the original.

134 Prater Stadium 1929-31
ERICH OTTO SCHWEITZER
II, Prater & Meiereistrasse   U: Praterstern then streetcar I
Austria's largest stadium (72,000). A boldly exposed r.c. frame under the tribunes.

135 Municipal Grain Warehouse 1911-13   KARL KREPP
II, Handelskai   U: Vorgartenstrasse then bus 10A or 11A
A long and monumental piece of eight to nine storey reinforced concrete frame construction, symmetrical about a central tower of twelve storeys. Fine piece of industrial building, now hotel.

136 Siedlung am Freihof 1923-7
KARL SCHARTELMÜLLER
XXII, Polletstrasse, Kagraner Platz, Steinenteschstrasse
U: Zentrum Kagran
Vienna's largest cooperative settlement at twice the size of Mayer's no 20 (1,014 dwellings), but less radical socially, though physical effect of a virtually autonomous two storey town. Plain architecture of rectangular volumes and pitched roofs, with touches of rather Expressionist over-emphasis in the details.

137 Weissenböckstrasse Siedlung 1923, '28
FRANK KAYM, ALFONS HETMANEK
XI, Simmeringer Hauptstrasse, Weissenböckstrasse, Wilhelm Kress Platz   U: Karlsplatz then streetcar 71
Most whimsey and romantic of the early 20s low-rise suburban developments or Siedlungen. Steeply pitched red-tiled roofs, brickwork features and stucco with occasional touches of 'classicism' fragment and individualise each villa in a vocabulary often close to early-80s Post-Modern.

138 Crematorium 1922   CLEMENS HOLZMEISTER
XI, Simmeringer Hauptstrasse 337
U: Karlsplatz then streetcar 71
Inside the walls of the old Neugebäude. Good example of Holzmeister's belief that architecture should 'perform', theatrically, not just function practically. Strange half Moorish style of angular smoke tower over stepped base with zig-zag castellation and broad pointed entrance arch.

139 Lueger Memorial Church 1907-10   MAX HEGELE
XI, Simmeringer Hauptstrasse 234
U: Karlsplatz then streetcar 71
Reminiscent in form and volume of Wagner's Steinhof, built as memorial to his confrère in municipalising Vienna, Burgermeister Dr Karl Lueger (see pp 6-7). Detailed in a Jugendstil that is often closer to stripped classicism than Secession or Wiener Werkstätte mosaics. Contains Lueger's sarcophagus, and Werkstätte mosaics.

140 Rannersdorf Siedlung 1921   HEINRICH TESSENOW
Schwechat-Rannersdorf, Stankagasse 8-18
U: Karlsplatz then streetcar 71 then bus 71A; or train from Wien Mitte to Grosse Schwechat (best in car).
Only Viennese work of this somewhat romantically anti-urbanist leader of the Deutscher Werkbund, designed for employees of the State Brewery two years after his period of teaching in the city from 1913-19. Semi-detached houses of the simplest cubic form with low-pitched roofs, four windows on the street and entrances originally through the timber-clad sides. Fences between enclosing the kitchen-garden plots are now walls, and much else changed. Recognisable, but only worth the journey for enthusiasts.